Spirit Games

300 Fun Activities That Bring Children Comfort and Joy

Barbara Sher

ILLUSTRATIONS BY
Ralph Butler

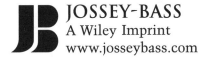
JOSSEY-BASS
A Wiley Imprint
www.josseybass.com

Copyright © 2002 by Barbara Sher. All rights reserved
Illustrations copyright © 2002 by Ralph Butler. All rights reserved

Design and production by Navta Associates, Inc.

Published by Jossey-Bass
A Wiley Imprint
989 Market Street, San Francisco, CA 94103-1741   www.josseybass.com

Published simultaneously in Canada

No part of this publication may be reproduced, stored in a retrieval system, or transmitted in any form or by any means, electronic, mechanical, photocopying, recording, scanning, or otherwise, except as permitted under Section 107 or 108 of the 1976 United States Copyright Act, without either the prior written permission of the publisher, or authorization through payment of the appropriate per-copy fee to the Copyright Clearance Center, Inc., 222 Rosewood Drive, Danvers, MA 01923, 978-750-8400, fax 978-646-8600, or on the Web at www.copyright.com. Requests to the publisher for permission should be addressed to the Permissions Department, John Wiley & Sons, Inc., 111 River Street, Hoboken, NJ 07030, 201-748-6011, fax 201-748-6008, or online at http://www.wiley.com/go/permissions.

Limit of Liability/Disclaimer of Warranty: While the publisher and author have used their best efforts in preparing this book, they make no representations or warranties with respect to the accuracy or completeness of the contents of this book and specifically disclaim any implied warranties of merchantability or fitness for a particular purpose. No warranty may be created or extended by sales representatives or written sales materials. The advice and strategies contained herein may not be suitable for your situation. You should consult with a professional where appropriate. Neither the publisher nor author shall be liable for any loss of profit or any other commercial damages, including but not limited to special, incidental, consequential, or other damages.

The publisher and the author have made every reasonable effort to insure that the experiments and activities in the book are safe when conducted as instructed but assume no responsibility for any damage caused or sustained while performing the experiments or activities in this book. Parents, guardians, and/or teachers should supervise young readers who undertake the experiments and activities in this book.

Readers should be aware that Internet Web sites offered as citations and/or sources for further information may have changed or disappeared between the time this was written and when it is read.

Jossey-Bass books and products are available through most bookstores. To contact Jossey-Bass directly call our Customer Care Department within the U.S. at 800-956-7739, outside the U.S. at 317-572-3986, or fax 317-572-4002.

Jossey-Bass also publishes its books in a variety of electronic formats. Some content that appears in print may not be available in electronic books.

ISBN: 0-471-40678-3

Printed in the United States of America
FIRST EDITION
PB Printing   10 9 8 7 6 5 4 3 2

Spirit Games

This book is dedicated to the spirit of
Richard Truman Skelton
because of all the time he "jollied"
me into a better mood.

Acknowledgments

To acknowledge the people who helped write this book would mean thanking all the people in my life, including and especially all the children from Nicaragua to Cambodia and countries in between who played games with me. Their enthusiasm was contagious and affirming.

I want to specifically thank my precious friends and coworkers in Saipan, Micronesia: Jane Bolton-Bound, for sharing her spirited parenting style and home-schooled children Tyler, Jesse, Jya and Louie; Jenny Slack for her sensitive and grounded awareness; Patty Staal for her loving competence; Mark Staal and son Kai for their appreciation of the fun factor; and Betty McDonald for being so quick to play. More appreciation to Jill Derickson, for her empathic caring, and Suzanne Lizama for giving me plenty of headroom. Thanks to teachers Batsa, Dora, Manny, Alex, Rita, Bobbi, Zena, Miercy, Antonia, Mae, and others, and the adorable children in the Head Start programs who made my heart sing by singing and playing with me.

Thank you to my daughters for their help: Jessica for her discerning proofreading, Roxanne for the deep sweetness of her support, Marissa for her clever insights. They have been a constant source of love and inspiration—and have wonderful mates, Stewart, Richard, and Mark. I am grateful to have a loving family and forever friends, namely Bonnie Wilson, Shirley Sher, Monty Sher, Glo Harris, Trisha and David Ferlic, Joan Becker, Cindy Taylor, Lorraine Carolan, Devlin and Eliza Grace Madrone, Jen Jones, Karen Beardsley, Sarah Dowell, Erica Storre, Sasu Donald, Shirley Gray, Toni Ross, Joani Rose, and the equally wonderful others in my extended family of Southern Humboldt County. They are people who have been there for me during good times and what we call A.F.G.O. times (Another Friggin' Growing Opportunity!).

Thank you to Wiley managing editor John Simko, copyeditor Miriam Sarzin, and Ralph Butler for his charming illustrations. And always, big BIG thanks to my absolutely favorite editor, Carole Hall.

I am grateful for them all.

Contents - - - - - - - - - - - - - - - -

Spirit
Games

Introduction: The Benefits of Joy ⌣ ⌣ ⌣

Joy is our natural state. You only have to look at the delighted face of an infant to know that we come prepackaged with an enormous sense of well-being. As children grow, that same state of well-being helps them to think with clarity, deal with problems, and reach out to others with love.

Spirit games are tools for creating such joy. They help children get past anger, get over self-doubt, and deal with sadness. They encourage feelings of compassion and show how to make a good day even better. There is evidence that by making children feel brighter and happier, spirit games can even prevent illness. Extensive studies have shown that prolonged dark feelings actually harm the body and can lead to disease.

Children's feelings are powerful. In my own family, I have seen a simple word of anger passed like a baton from one member to the next until the whole house was upset. Likewise, one simple act of love has permeated everyone. While we can't deny that negative feelings and painful experiences are part of the human condition, most of us feel more in sync with the world when we are giving or experiencing joy.

Spirit games let children have fun doing the serious business of evolving into ever-expanding sources of smiles. These activities provide abundant ways to feel tuned in, happy, appreciated, and appreciative.

SPIRIT GAMES FOR YOU

This book starts with games designed for only you to play. There is a simple reason for this: one of the best ways to help our children to be happy is to be happy ourselves. We are our children's best role models. Rarely taught in school or honed at home, the ability to lift your own spirit is one of the greatest gifts you can give your child.

Like any other discipline, feeling good takes practice and the continual gathering of useful skills. Fortunately, we never lose our ability to learn. Did you know that human beings have over five thousand thoughts a day?

All those thoughts give us plenty of opportunity to practice the art of feeling good!

Let me help you practice. For example, start your day off in a positive mood with quick games such as Joy Practice and Setting the Scene.

Games such as Mother Yourself and You Are Annoying, So I Bless You will help you deal with difficult moments and guide you past them.

And Frame Each Year will teach you a mode of keeping in touch with the feeling that all is well.

SPIRIT GAMES FOR CHILDREN

Whenever you wish, share the rest of the games and activities in this book with the children in your life. Some of the games are designed to bring comfort and joy during trying aspects of a child's emotional life: times of sadness, self-doubt, anger, or fear. Other games expand children's capacity for compassion, sharing joy, and manifesting magic.

Almost all of the games in this book have proven to be fun for children of all ages. Some are especially appropriate for families. For example:

▶ Expect quick pick-me-up smiles from games like Do A 360 and Joy Juicer Words.

▶ Practice setting the tone for the day with Say Something Nice Day and The Thank Bank.

▶ Experience your power to make someone's day with A Garland of Wishes and You've Got Mail.

▶ Create meaningful family experiences to share again and again with games such as Keeping Track of the Miracles and Rise Up Singing.

SPIRIT GAMES FOR YOUNG ONES

Two- to Seven-Year-Olds

Certain games work especially well at meeting common needs and preferences for fun at different developmental stages. For example, our very young ones live so in-the-moment that their moods can change instantly from extreme joy to demanding anger. When they confront us with this volatility, we have two choices: we can respond in kind or we can change their focus.

Games like Finding the Grumpy Bug and Mom's Gone Nuts can help you change the mood. Then the most wondrous thing happens. By tapping into our children's ability to shift into another gear, we get to see the sparkle return to their eyes and, as our hearts melt, our own moods lighten.

Games for young ones are mutually beneficial. We can more easily work out whatever needs to be worked out from this loving space that the games enable us to create together.

Games for this age also show a fun way of looking at life, as in Hello Mr. Chair/Hello Ms. Pot and I Notice. You will also be encouraging cooperation with games such as Race against Time and Your Honorable Head Garbage Taker-Outer.

SPIRIT GAMES FOR THE MIDDLE ONES

Eight- to Twelve-Year-Olds

During the middle years, while we parents still hold a special place, peer pressure begins to influence our children's spirits. So some of the best games for this age help children to stay in touch with their own feelings, such as Feeling Faces and How Is Your Garden Today?

Other games explore ways of dealing with outside influences, among them Choices, Choices Everywhere, while games like Walk in My Shoes encourage compassion for others.

Some of your favorites may turn out to be the games that help keep the sweet connection between you and yours alive, such as Love Breaths and While You Sleep.

Thirteen- to Fifteen-Year-Olds

Young teenagers have a strong sense of self, even if it's sometimes riddled with insecurity and doubt, so many of these games are designed to increase their trust in themselves and in their own inner wisdom. For this purpose, try games such as Intuition Exercises and Magic Collage.

Other games in this section encourage trust in a higher wisdom, such as One Door Closes, Another Door Opens and Ask for a Sign.

Games to enhance a teenager's sense of his or her own history are Every Thing Talks a Story and Memory Jar.

You will also find games for sharing kindness with others, such as The Healing Circle and Enchanted Cloaks Last Forever.

SPIRIT GAMES FOR OLDER TEENS

Sixteen-Year-Olds and Up

As we get older, we start to understand that the only thing we can have total control over is our attitude. Many of these games give our older children tools for adjusting their attitudes, such as Change the Energy and Dream BIG.

Our children at this age remind us of blooming flowers. They are all fragile in their own way. You can help them deal with heartbreak with games such as A Notebook of Good-bye and It's Crying Time. You can help them stay connected to their capacity for joy with Present Moment/Wonderful Moment.

LET YOUR CHILDREN COMFORT YOU, TOO

It's one thing to help your child; it's quite another to be brave enough to share yourself with your children and let them help you from time to time. But it's usually worth the risk. For example, my daughters have given me very good parenting advice. Oldest daughter Jessica's advice about consistent bedtimes for her younger sisters helped us all.

Another bit of helpful advice came from middle daughter Roxanne when she was five years old and had gotten very frustrated when her little sister wanted to play with her dolls and wouldn't obey her and play Roxanne's game. She got mean. When I chastised her and comforted her sister, she explained to me that I was doing it wrong. "I wouldn't yell at Marissa if I weren't having a bad time. So you should comfort me."

It made sense and the next time it happened, I took her in my arms and rocked her, saying: "Oh, you must be having a hard time. You are such a nice little girl that I am sure you wouldn't be mean unless you were unhappy. Poor baby."

Her little sister didn't seem to mind my giving attention to Roxanne because it meant that she could go back to playing with her dolls in peace. Roxanne, feeling comforted and seen for the whole person she was, slowly returned to her nice self and got down from my lap and we all felt better.

Giving children permission to talk to you without fear of being censured gives them the necessary knowledge that their feelings and ideas matter.

GETTING READY TO PLAY

▶ All of the games for children can be played with children of either sex, regardless of the gender of the children in the instructions or illustrations.

▶ Almost all of the games can be played by two willing players—you and your child.

▶ If the instructions of an intriguing game are written for a group, remember that you can always modify the rules a bit to fit just the two of you.

▶ Some of the games work especially well with groups. These games are coded with a ◯. If you have a growing family, are a classroom teacher or volunteer, a play group leader, a camp counselor—or are organizing a birthday party or a family gathering—you will enjoy playing around with these ideas.

▶ Remember, there are no wrong ways to do these games. Any response is perfect and personal.

▶ There are many variations of some of the games because learning the same lessons in many ways makes them "stick to the ribs" better. Also, discovering different ways to learn the same things increases a child's acceptance of variations. If a game inspires you to do a variation of it that you make up, great! Do it!

The best setting for the various games is always the same: a playful, safe place where being oneself is the best thing to be.

THE BEST TIME TO PLAY

We have only a brief while to establish a positive influence over our children's lives. Seize the moments while your children are young, and leave the dishes and laundry for later.

The best time to play is whenever the mood strikes you. On a rainy day, when friends are over, when you want to linger a little longer around the dinner table, at birthday parties, or instead of TV, play a game. When you are driving in the car and want to distract siblings from their arguments or their complaints about being bored, play a game. Play when your children are in a high-energy mood on one of your low-energy days.

Pick the game that fits the mood. You might want to have a regular game time that the children can count on.

Browse through and see which games appeal to you and jot down a word or two to jog your memory or the titles and page numbers. Stick your list on the refrigerator to help you remember.

PART ONE

Spirit Games for You

Chapter 1

NURTURING YOUR SPIRIT

Joy Practice

"Happiness is not a state to arrive at, but a manner of traveling."

—Margaret Lee Runbeck

Taking time for yourself, even if it's only five minutes each day, is not self-indulgence, it is self-respect.

DIRECTIONS

Develop a personal ritual for starting each day with an inner smile.

Examples

◇ Sit in the sunniest morning spot with a hot cup of coffee, milk, or tea and look out the window admiring any beauty in the surroundings or sky.

◇ Stretch languorously and appreciate your health.

◇ Allow time for a daydream as big as you can possibly imagine.

◇ Chat with your God or higher self or personal guides or angels.

◇ Write in a journal without censoring.

◇ Be grateful for anything that is going well.

◇ Pray and/or meditate.

◇ Ground yourself by visualizing a root going from your tailbone deep into the center of the earth.

◇ Breath consciously. (Think "I am breathing in; I am breathing out" and notice the space between the "in" breath and the "out" breath.)

◇ Take a walk in nature or sit by water.

For You

Ways to Walk

Being in the present moment is the ideal state, but it's easy to get distracted by yesterday's news and tomorrow's fears. I find walking can be a good time to practice being in the now. I play this little series of games because they help me stay there.

DIRECTIONS

Switch back and forth between these games in whatever order you want.

1. *Call Off the Thought Police:* During this period allow whatever thoughts want to come into your head—anything. Feel free to obsess, grumble, fantasize.

2. *Feel the Ground:* Pay close attention to how your feet feel when they make contact with the ground. Notice bumps and inclines.

3. *Hear All the Sounds:* Listen carefully for sounds and name them. "That's the wind going through the trees. That's an engine starting up."

Whether they are wonderful sounds or annoying sounds, stay objective and just name them.

4. *Feel the Air:* Which direction is the wind coming from? Feel it on your face. If the air is moving slowly, you might need to turn slowly in a circle to feel where it is coming from. (Unless turning circles where you are will look a bit odd!)

5. *Count Your Steps:* If you have a long way to walk, break it up into smaller goals. Guess how many steps it will take to get to that house or tree or street—two hundred steps? fifty? Start counting and see how accurate your guess was. Do it for the next chunk of your walk and see if your guess is closer.

6. *Count Your Breaths:* Be aware of your "in" breath and your "out" breath. Don't force your breath to a certain pattern, just think, "I am breathing in, number one. I am breathing out, number one. I am breathing in, number two. I am breathing out, number two," and so on.

See how many breaths you can count before being distracted by a different thought. Can you make it to ten? Twenty? Much more? Much less? Keep trying for your personal best.

For You

Messages from Nature

I remember how delighted I was the time I saw a baby water snake try to make it up a tiny waterfall and fail a few times before succeeding. All creatures in nature, including us, have to go through a learning process.

Once I watched as a spider made the first line of a new web by hanging from a single thread for a while before a breeze came along and swung it to another branch. Watching the process reminded me to wait patiently before starting a new project and trust that the "winds of fate" will blow me in the right direction.

DIRECTIONS

When you go for a walk, keep an eye out for something that attracts you and then make up what that could mean for your day.

There are no right or wrong meanings. Be truly personal and intuitive.

Examples

◇ If you see a fallen leaf and are struck with how beautiful it is, imagine what that might mean to you and why it so attracts you today. Noticing fallen leaves might mean that you are beginning to see that there is beauty in gracefully letting go of something when it is over.

◇ If a wildflower attracts you it might mean that you are seeing the specialness in just being however you naturally are.

◇ If you are fascinated by watching butterflies today, it might mean that you are longing for more freedom.

VARIATION

♦ Notice what scenes happen in front of you and what they might mean to you.

Examples

◇ Walking in the park, you are fascinated by the ways some children get so much entertainment value out of playing with a stick. It makes you realize that you need more fun in your life and you decide to make some time for that in your schedule.

◇ You overhear a shopkeeper berate her employee in an effort to improve his work and you see the devastated look on the employee's face. You realize that there is a way in which you criticize your child that is not beneficial to her self-esteem and you decide to explore gentler ways of helping her growth.

〜〜〜〜〜〜〜〜〜〜〜〜〜〜〜〜〜〜〜〜〜〜 For You

Feeling Moments

Describing feelings as moments reminds us that feelings are transitory. It also helps reinforce the notion of appreciating the pleasant moments, which are also impermanent.

DIRECTIONS

Practice describing your feelings as moments. The next time you are feeling particularly happy or sad, tell yourself, "I am having a _____ moment." Fill in the blank with the word that best matches your feeling.

Examples

◇ I am having an anxious moment.

◇ I am having an envious moment

◇ I am having a neighborly moment.

◇ I am having a stupidity moment.

◇ I am having a joyous moment.

〜〜〜〜〜〜〜〜〜〜〜〜〜〜〜〜〜〜〜〜〜〜 For You

Setting the Scene

When my children were growing up, I had a small table in my bedroom on which I would set a tableau of little figures. I made figures for each family member and our pets. I added things I found or collected, and gave each a meaning. A small turtle sculpture was to remember to take things slowly. An otter was to symbolize "finding the fun."

Every so often, I would change my little scene. I might put a little duck next to the child who needed to let a recent negative experience roll off like water off a duck's back. I might put an angel next to the child who was going on a school outing.

The making of the tableaus would calm me as I took the time to think about what I wished for the people I love. And if things went as I had wished, I could give myself some of the credit!

DIRECTIONS

Materials

oven-bake clay and assorted objects

Make little sculptures of whoever is "family" to you. Let your children help you if you want. Use clay that hardens in the oven or in the air. Don't worry about realism—just loving that person while you're making it will make it perfect.

Scout around in the house or outside or at garage sales or novelty shops for little things that you can give your own meaning to. A rock could mean you are wanting life to be more stable. A feather could mean you are wanting to float along with what is happening rather than resist.

Put all your figures in a box next to or under a small table.

Make a tableau with the figures in your family. Place around each figure the objects that symbolize what you are wanting for them now and what they are wanting for themselves. Don't forget to add symbolic figures for what you are hoping for yourself as well.

Changing the tableau fairly often keeps the energy fresh.

Examples

◇ A dog might mean that you want comfort for whoever the dog is next to in the tableau.

◇ A turtle might mean that you want that person who is traveling to feel as "at home" as the creatures that carry their house with them.

◇ A cat might mean you want the person to be unconcerned with the opinions of others.

◇ An egg might mean wanting a new start at something.

◇ A spiritual figure might mean wanting guidance.

VARIATION

♦ Instead of using figures, use photos and pictures and other "hangable" items.

String up a ribbon and use clothespins to attach photos of family members. Beside each photo, hang a picture of what you are wishing for that person.

Examples

◇ Hang a beach picture by the person you would like to see become more relaxed.

◇ Hang a dollar bill next to the person whose fortune you'd like to see expanded.

◇ Hang a green leaf next to the person whose new growth in some area needs recognition.

For You

Frame Each Year

At the end of each year, as my children grew, I made a photo collage.

It was interesting and enjoyable to go through the photos that were piled up in a shoebox and pick the ones that best showed the highlights of that year. By its nature, this experience emphasized the positive aspects of the year. Few "Kodak moments" occur during difficult times.

DIRECTIONS

During the holidays or even after the new year starts, bring out all your photos from the year.

Pick out the ones that best show aspects of the year.

Put them all together in a pleasing arrangement or a collage.

Materials

photos and frame

Put them in a large picture frame and label it with the year shown. (A photo of someone's birthday cake can mark the year.)

Hang your collage on a wall with collages from previous years.

For You

You Are Annoying, So I Bless You

I lived on a county road that used to have hardly any traffic. As the population grew, so did the traffic noise. When I sat outside, I'd get irritated with the car sounds until I discovered this game: Bless everyone.

When I started to feel irritation come up as a car went by, I turned my annoyance instead to a blessing. I blessed the people going by and wished that they got to their destination safely. Since my road leads to the ocean, I imagined that they were going to have fun.

DIRECTIONS

When someone or something is irritating or annoying or scary, look for a way in which you could change the focus by finding something to bless. Say the blessing silently to yourself.

Examples

◊ Someone cuts ahead of you in line: "I bless you with feeling good about yourself so that you don't feel the need to be first."

◊ Car passes in the left lane and is going way too fast, especially if it cuts you off or scares you: "I bless you with calmness so that you can get in touch with what is important and drive better."

◊ Big semi comes up close behind you and momentarily scares you and then passes you: "I bless you with compassion for others so you will be careful not to scare people."

◊ Someone at work is very grumpy and taking it out on his subordinates: "May you find peace."

Mother Yourself

"When you become aware of misjudgment, ill-timed, ill-conceived thoughts and actions, when you recognize your desire for vengeance, your anger or unforgiveness, that is the time for self-congratulations. Your insight now allows you to handle these things in a far more conscious way."

—*Emmanuel*

Regardless of the nature of the mothering you've had, you can still tuck an ideal, loving mother inside your heart to be nice to you when you need it.

My daughter Marissa suggested this game to me at a time when I was being unnecessarily harsh with myself. "Mother yourself," she said kindly. "I highly recommend you."

DIRECTIONS

When you are having a hard time, try these steps:

1. See the wound that caused the pain and tell the mother in you what happened. (Example: "My coworker spoke so harshly to me. I felt like she doesn't respect me.")

2. Dress the wound by giving yourself the empathy that a loving mom might have given you. ("Oh, that must have really hurt your feelings. Poor baby.")

3. Find the words that would comfort you. ("Maybe she wasn't really mad at you. Perhaps she is having a hard time and let it out on you because she feels safe with you." Even if it's true that she doesn't respect you, can you see that as only her opinion and really not your business? Do *you* respect you? That's what is important.)

4. Give yourself love and attention in all the ways that you'd like. ("I am sorry that living life hurts sometimes. You are so precious and you are doing so well. How wise of you to have compassion for your friend. Would you like to do something that will make you feel better. Wanna go for a walk?")

For You ˏ ˎ ˏ ˎ ˏ ˎ ˏ ˎ ˏ ˎ ˏ ˎ ˏ ˎ ˏ ˎ ˏ ˎ ˏ ˎ ˏ

Mirror, Mirror

During one particularly intense period, I was rehearsing for a dance performance at the same time I was preparing for a large workshop, and my husband was in a hospital that was a two-hour drive away. I was either madly trying to remember dance steps or scribbling away at preparation notes or driving to an emotional scene.

All's well that ends well, however. My husband got better, I remembered the dance steps, and my workshop was a great success. I was feeling so proud of myself that when I looked in the mirror the day it was all over, I smiled at myself and said, "Good job, Barbara."

It was shocking.

I had never seen myself look like that in the mirror. I am more used to brief looks of criticism as I poke at blemishes or jab at unruly hair.

This smiling person with love shining out of her eyes had a face that my children must see when they insist that to them I am beautiful. Since that experience, I have made a point when passing a mirror to smile genuinely at myself.

DIRECTIONS

Materials
mirror

Purposely look in the mirror and smile lovingly at yourself and say some nice things. Look at yourself as if you were looking at someone you adore.

Turn any critical thoughts into a compliment: "I am weird looking" becomes "I have a unique and interesting face." "I have wrinkles" becomes "I have laugh lines."

Look at yourself as if at your best friend, and share that look that says, "We're in this together and we are going to be just fine."

For You

Face Language

We can learn a lot about others and ourselves by reading facial cues. This game remind us that, like artists, we are slowly etching the lines on our faces with our thoughts. If we want to know what people's main thoughts have been in their lives, we don't have to read "between the lines"—we can just read the lines.

Materials

mirror

DIRECTIONS

Try out various expressions in the mirror to see how they form different lines in your face.

Examples

◇ Feel scared and excited and raise your eyebrows as if you were saying, "Oh, gosh, look what's happening to me. Am I going to be able to handle this?" Notice how it makes parallel lines on your forehead.

◇ Feel pathetic, hurt, and angry, as if you were saying, "Why me? They are hurting me again." Or "Damn—I'm going to get you for this." Notice how it makes vertical lines in the space between your eyebrows.

◇ Feel disdainful and sniff up as if smelling something slightly off. Notice the lines that come down from the sides of your nose.

◇ Feel annoyed and hold your lips very tight together, as if you'd like to say something nasty but aren't. Notice the tiny lines that form around your mouth.

◇ Stick your lower lip out and pout and see how that drapes the skin around your chin.

◇ Feel happy and give a big broad smile, as if you were very pleased. Notice the laugh lines around the outside of your eyes that are caused by the cheek muscles pushing up and squishing the skin there.

◇ Experiment with other expressions and see how they show on your face.

◇ If you already have some lines on your face, exaggerate them to see if you can tell what kinds of thoughts would produce those lines.

For You

Talking to the Future

This game helped me decide a major move. My future self said, "It's going to be better than you can imagine." I made the move and I ended up so glad about my choice.

This may not be as far-fetched as it sounds; quantum physicists are now telling us that time is not sequential and that past, present, and future are all happening at once. To grasp this, I find it helpful to think of my life as a vertical pole rather than a horizontal line. My younger self is at the bottom; my future self is at the top. This way I can go up or down the pole and contact any one of them.

DIRECTIONS

Set up two chairs: one for you and one for your future self. Ask the question(s) that she wants answered, such as:

"Is this a good decision?"

"Will I like having gone there?"

"Should I do that?"

"Should I do it all?"

Then be very still and listen to whatever answer comes into your head. It may feel as if the answers are being made up; that's okay. If the advice feels "right," that is what matters.

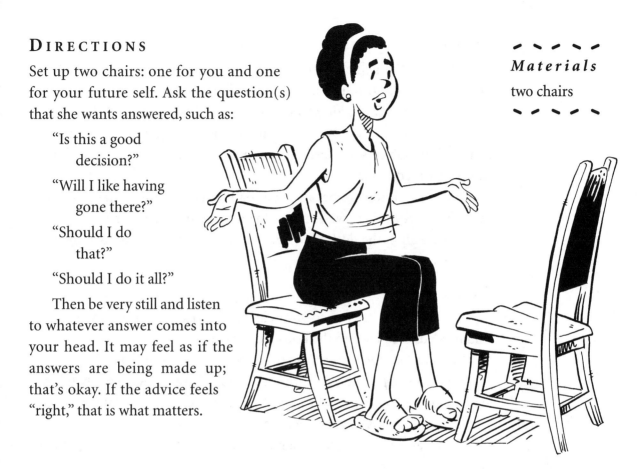

Materials

two chairs

- For You

Fanciful Perspectives

It's well known that ten witnesses to one scene may come up with ten different versions of what happened. Depending upon your point of view, you can see any circumstance in many different ways.

DIRECTIONS

Recall the last time that something annoyed you. What was your perspective on what happened? Now imagine other, fanciful perspectives to explain what happened. Change perspectives until you find one that makes you feel better. It doesn't matter whether that version is "true" or not.

Example

Situation: Someone pulled out into the traffic in front of you, making you have to slow down to accommodate him.

Your original perspective: You thought that driver was a selfish jerk.

Fanciful perspectives: You were a noble and compassionate queen. One of your little subjects was feeling anxious and needed to scurry ahead. You graciously made room.

You were all worker bees on the road together and one more joined your group. Now there were more of you to get the work done.

You are all in the flow of a river. Watch out for rocks and darting fish (cars that pull in front of you!).

Example

Situation: On the way to your car, you realized you forgot your keys and needed to go back to the house to get them.

Your original perspective: You thought you were going to be late.

Fanciful perspectives: By forgetting your keys, you were really taking part in the larger scheme of things. By being a few minutes late, you gave someone else your space on the road.

How clever you were to remember the keys before you actually got all the way to the car!

Example

Situation: Your child just broke a favorite dish of yours.

Your original perspective: You were angry and at the breaking point yourself. You yelled at your child, but you felt bad about it later.

Fanciful perspectives: You had a wonderful opportunity to realize the unimportance of material objects. Next time, you won't explode. You learned something that will help you choose your child's self-esteem over an object.

You just got an excuse to buy some other piece that will please you.

Example

Situation: You smiled at someone who didn't return your smile.

Fanciful perspectives: The person is "happy challenged," which is a serious handicap, and needs a prayer said for him. "May he find happiness."

You are both in a play. That person had the grumpy part and was being such a good actor by staying true to his part and not "breaking character."

For You

Guided Writing

This is not a game that speaks to everyone, but it will speak strongly to some and be a positive addition to a daily meditation practice.

DIRECTIONS

Write down a question with your dominant hand (if you are right-handed, use your right hand).

Then sit quietly for a little while. Try and "get out of the way" and not anticipate what the answer will be. With your nondominant hand, write down the words that come to you. Concentrate on writing legibly. Let whatever words or images come.

If the response feels pleasant and helpful, continue. If not, simply stop and turn your attention elsewhere.

Materials

pen and paper
or journal

VARIATION

◆ If you get comfortable with this game and learn how to listen, you don't need to use your nondominant hand anymore. Just write what you "hear" as a kind of meditation practice.

`⌄ ⌄ ⌄ ⌄ ⌄ ⌄ ⌄ ⌄ ⌄ ⌄ ⌄ ⌄ ⌄ ⌄ ⌄`

Vacuum Back Your Power

One day I was walking along the beach feeling fine when I began to pass a few people who were sitting on the sand. I suddenly started worrying about how I looked to them. I wondered if my hair was a mess and felt embarrassed that I was dressed more for comfort than style. In one second I went from feeling good to feeling bad.

I had given away my power. I had given those strangers the power to decide my worth at that moment.

The reality is that those people probably weren't even aware of me at all. I laughed at myself and consciously took back my power and continued my walk in my previous good humor.

You can easily give your power away and feel defeated. In this game, you take it back.

DIRECTIONS

The next time you suddenly feel defeated and feel that someone else has a negative view of you, or at the end of the day notice you are feeling bad about yourself, play this game.

1. Review the day or moment when you let someone else's opinion of you matter more than yours. It could have been just a passing moment, as in a look of disdain from a passenger on the subway. It could have been a salesperson or your supervisor. It could have been one person or many in a day. In this part of the game, just notice who it was and when it happened and imagine that every time it happened, you left a little shadow of yourself behind.

2. Next, sit down in a quiet space and imagine your body has a giant vacuum hose or you have an enormous magnet (whichever image you

prefer) and suck or magnetize back to yourself the little shadows of yourself that got left behind. Go back to each situation and consciously take back the part of you that got left there.

3. As you begin to feel more expanded and solid and in a better-feeling place, remember that your opinion of yourself matters enormously. It is only when you are loving you that you are able to best love others.

⁀ ⁀ ⁀ ⁀ ⁀ ⁀ ⁀ ⁀ ⁀ ⁀ ⁀ ⁀ ⁀ ⁀ ⁀ ⁀   For You

A Feeling Collage

Getting in touch with feelings can be difficult. Often we numb ourselves because we don't want to experience uncomfortable or painful feelings. Ironically, we sometimes also avoid feelings of joy or self-satisfaction because we have been taught that we don't deserve them when others aren't happy or that we will get a "big head." But feelings are our best guides to how we are doing. If the feelings are dark, we need to be aware of them in order to get past them—often the best way out is through. When our feelings are positive, we need to savor them. Keep this collage in view to remind you of pleasing feelings.

DIRECTIONS

Look through magazines, catalogs, old greeting cards and calendars, etc. Find pictures that appeal to you at that moment. ("I like this picture of a lake because I would just love right now to be floating on my back in water and not worrying about anything.")

Cut or tear out the pictures and place them in whatever arrangement feels right to you. Glue them on a piece of cardboard.

Materials

magazines, catalogs, greeting cards, newspaper, scissors, glue, cardboard or poster board

For You

The Enchantment of Water

Once I was working with an autistic child. He expressed fleeting interest in the bag of toys I brought, but otherwise he kept his face passive and was uninterested in me.

When I heard he liked to be in the sea, I asked his mom to bring him to the beach one day. For an hour we "played" together. He reached for me. We splashed each other. He imitated my making sand cakes. And I got more eye contact from him in that one hour than I did in all the months before. Water has incredible healing powers.

DIRECTIONS

Materials

water

Go find some water to sit by, sit in, or move through. Share your worries with it.

Examples

◊ Sitting by moving water, such as a river or running brook, take a leaf and put your troubles on it and watch it float away.

◊ At a large body of water, such as a pond or lake, throw in pebbles or huge rocks, one by one. Name each one for a pesky problem, and throw each one away with force; watch its ripples diminish and notice how the water returns to calm.

◊ Swimming through the water, count your strokes, and don't think about anything except how silky the water feels against your skin.

◊ Standing in a shower, imagine that troubles wash right off.

◊ Soaking in a tub, let your anxieties go down the drain.

◊ Drinking water, imagine the flow flushing out dark feelings.

◊ If you have a bucket of water, throw it down the outside stairs along with those worrisome thoughts.

PART TWO

Spirit Games for Children

Chapter 2

MORE JOY, PLEASE!

Put Everything in a Pile

I had been out of town for a week, leaving the children in the loving and competent hands of their father. When I got back, the girls were well fed and well loved, but I had to wade through seven days of strewn clothes, game parts, leftover stale toast, and other questionables to get to them.

I was too glad to be home to be mad, so I decided to approach the overwhelming task by putting everything, regardless of what it was, into a large pile in the middle of the room and then sorting it out one by one.

Borrowing the tune from "The Bear Went Over the Mountain," I sang and they sang with me:

"Put everything in a pile
Put everything in a pile
Put everything in a p-i-l-e
In the middle of the room.
The middle of the room,
The middle of the room,
Put everything in a p-i-l-e
In the middle of the room."

My five-year-old was suspicious that this was a work game, but she also knew that the work was going to be done. The choice was the hard way or the fun way.

So, tossing and singing, the work went fairly quickly, and soon the edges of the room were cleaned and in the middle was this huge mound. We sat around it as if at a campfire. Then, in a rhythmic sing-song, I held up the first item and said, "A sock, a sock, oh where does it go?" Soon the

large pile was reduced to separate smaller piles of laundry, books, trash, sweater, etc., and everyone was assigned a pile to put away while I swept the floor.

The house was habitable again and we were all still in good moods.

DIRECTIONS

When you have a very messy area to clean up, like your child's room, play this game.

All players toss everything onto the bed that was on the floor or draped over the chairs or teetering on the shelves. *Everything!* (You grab the not-to-be-tossed stuff first and put it out of the way.) Keep tossing until the room is tidy everywhere except for the mound of stuff on the bed. Children don't seem to mind tossing things, so this part of the game goes quickly. With very young children it helps to sing a little song to help them maintain their focus, and with older ones, songs make the work go better because everyone is in the same rhythm.

The tidiness of the edges of the room can serve as an inspiration to move on with the next task of sorting things out.

Pick up each item and chant something like:

"A book, a book, where does it go?" and someone goes and puts it on the bookshelf.

Continue with each thing until the bed is empty.

Make the bed and walk out of the room, and celebrate with a hot cup of cocoa or a cold fruit smoothie.

Young Ones

Crazy Day

Doing different things expands who we are and increases our enjoyment of life. Learning to play a flute or traveling are ways we do this. But we can also do it in a simple way by doing everyday things differently.

DIRECTIONS

Declare the day "Crazy Day." Invite your child to join you in celebrating it by doing a few or a lot of things differently than usual.

Examples

◊ Say good night when you wake up in the morning.

◊ Eat your eggs with a spoon.

◊ Have pancakes for dinner.

◊ Eat with your nondominant hand. (If you're right-handed, eat with your left.)

◊ Wear your socks on your ears.

◊ Walk backwards to the store.

◊ Say your names backwards. Mark is Kram. Kai is Iak.

◊ Eat dessert first!

Young Ones

Race against Time

Have you ever had trouble getting kids to cooperate? Have you noticed how they go a little more quickly than they otherwise might when you've added a challenge to the mix? Children who weren't even fooled by my real motive still liked beating the clock.

"Let's see if you can run upstairs and get your shoes and be back down by the count of seven."

This strategy works on adults, too. One night I was driving home from a trip. The kids had been cranky and fussy for a long while and I wasn't feeling much better myself. I blew up and started yelling.

"Mom," my five-year-old said calmly and sincerely, "let's see if you can calm down by the time I count to seven." She began counting. As she saw my face relax and my mouth curl up in amusement, she said, "Good, Mom. You did it by six!"

This game is much different than the "I'll give you to ten to get those shoes or you know what" threat.

It's a race against time.

It's a challenge of speed and agility and remembering what we are supposed to do at the end.

DIRECTIONS

Start the game like this:

"Let's see if you can run upstairs, get your coat, and come back down before I get to the number six. Ready? Set? Go! One . . . Two . . . Three. . . Four . . . Five . . . Five and a half . . . Five and three quarters . . . Six. You Made It!"

For older players, you can add more requests, such as:

"Let's see if you can run upstairs, get your coat, put it on, and get out to the car before the number seventeen."

VARIATIONS

♦ Use the game for pure fun purposes, too. "Let's see how fast you can run around the swings, touch the big tree, and come back. Can you do it by thirty-six? Ready? Go!"

♦ Use it to get a portion of a child's room cleaned. Do only a portion at a time. It makes the game go quicker and one neat area can inspire the desire to make another. (It's a trick I use on myself.) Using a timer, say, "Let's see if you can get these toy shelves straightened up before the bell rings." Actually, when the task looks overwhelming, this game works better if you say "Let see how fast *we* can . . ."

Your Honorable Head Garbage Taker-Outer

As long as we have to clean the house anyway and get our children to do their part, we might as well make it feel like the important work it really is. We can do it the way big corporations do—give everyone a title.

I discovered this game when trying to bolster some enthusiasm for a gardening project. The minute I gave out titles, everyone burst into activity.

DIRECTIONS

Confer a title on each person and for each aspect of a task. Instead of asking "Would you please grate the potatoes," say, "You can be the Great Grater."

Examples

◊ Children helping in the garden become:

Honorable Hole Maker

Splendid Seed Putter-Inner

Super Seed Cover-Upper

◊ Children helping in the kitchen become:

Majesty Mixer

Princess Table Setter

King Sweeper

Young Ones

Marching Mikey and Jumping Jessie

If you are in the mood to be silly . . .

DIRECTIONS

Each person takes turn saying his name and adding an action to it. It's fun to make it rhyme with your name even if it isn't a word.

Then everyone makes that same movement all around the room, saying the name as they move.

Examples

◇ Babbling Barbara

◇ Marching Mikey

◇ Jittering Jennifer

◇ Jumping Jessie

◇ Tumbling Thorn

◇ "Jalloping" John

◇ Reeling Roger

Young Ones

I Notice Newness

When we have had to walk the same old walk many times in a row, I play this game to make it more interesting. What is surprising is how many new things you can see if you look for them.

DIRECTIONS

If you often take the same walk, like the walk to school or to the store, invite your child to help you see how many new things you each can notice.

Look for details that you might have missed. Maybe you never noticed before how the post holding up a mailbox had small carvings on it.

It could be something that wasn't there before, like the first crocus in spring.

When anyone sees something, say aloud, "I notice something new!" and the other player looks around and tries to find the newness, too. Clues can be given freely.

VARIATIONS

◆ Play the I Notice Newness game with your children as you drive a familiar route in the car. It can be a good way of occupying their attention in the car instead of listening to them squabbling with each other.

- Your child can play it on his way home from school and report to you all the new things he saw. Instead of asking, "What did you do at school today," you can ask, "What did you notice on your way home?"

- Look at a photograph or magazine picture for one minute. Notice lots of details. Then turn the photo over and all say how many things they remember. Write them down or just say them aloud. Then turn the photo back over and see if any were forgotten.

- Pick a particular spot in the house, like the coffee table or a cluttered desk or the refrigerator, and notice everything there. Players take turns closing their eyes or turning their backs and describing all that is there. Open your eyes or turn around and see how much is remembered.

- For the small child, put a few things on a plate and have her name them, and then cover the plate with a scarf and see how many of the things she can remember.

Young Ones

In the Same Breath

There's nothing sweeter than feeling "in sync" or "in tune" with another.

DIRECTIONS

Sit knee to knee with your little one and practice breathing exactly together. You will be surprised at how content and connected this game will make you feel.

Don't use words, just look at each other and slowly get in sync. Inhale in at the same time. Hold the breath for the same amount of time. Exhale and breathe out at the same time.

Try and match the amount of air taken in. A big breath involves the chest, and the stomach rises. A little breath just happens in the nose.

VARIATIONS

♦ Both breathe naturally and notice any difference in the length and depth of your inhales and exhales.

♦ Make up an unusual breathing pattern to do together, such as one deep breath followed by two shallow ones. Keep repeating the pattern.

♦ Hum together. Hum the same tone for a while and then experiment with finding different tones that harmonize and sound good together.

Young Ones

Shaping Clouds

Sometimes what is behind children's down moods is the sense that they are powerless. In this game we share with children that far from being powerless, they are so powerful that they can change the shape of the clouds.

DIRECTIONS

Lie outside on your backs and watch the clouds for a while. Then when each person is ready, she picks a cloud whose shape she is going to change. She can use just her mind to tell the cloud what shapes she wants it. She can imagine her magical arms reaching out and molding the cloud. Tuck this part in. Round this part. Turn it into a dinosaur.

Start small. Make a hole in the cloud. Make a wispy cloud disappear altogether. Feel yourselves feeling connected to everything in the universe.

Then lie very patiently and watch it happen. It does happen and it has happened for everyday folks like us (although it will probably happen faster for your child than for you, but you both can watch in amazement as her dinosaur appears in the sky).

Next time she is feeling sad and small, remind her of the time she was so powerful, she changed the shape of a cloud.

Dreamy Scribbles

Take the time to do this activity with your child. You might find that it calms you, too.

DIRECTIONS

Play some calming music on a CD or tape, or find a quiet music station on your radio. Listen to the music for a while with your child. Start to draw with one crayon each. Encourage each other not to look at the paper as you are drawing. Not looking helps you not to judge what you are doing as good or bad.

Materials

crayon, paper, calming music recordings

If your hand moves freely, you will probably make an abstract design. It's a dreamy experience. Then color in the spaces, if you wish.

Spaced in Your Space

Everyone needs a place to dream—a small space to crawl into for sweet solitude that feels calm and comforting—a place just right for dreaming.

DIRECTIONS

Look around your home with your child and find a little nook that feels just right, such as under a cloth-covered table or in a corner of the family room. Maybe you could pick up an empty appliance box and make little doors out of the carton's flaps.

Materials

personal items

After the space is found, see what your child wants to put into it. Pillow? Blanket? Colored pens and paper?

Fixing up a Dream Space with your children is a wonderful afternoon project that lets them know how much they are loved. It can last for a while or be taken down so you have the fun of doing it again.

VARIATIONS

Even if children have their own rooms, it can make them feel important to have a part of the family rooms to decorate.

◆ Each child gets a windowsill of his own that he can decorate with his beautiful found objects, such as a special rock, a special shell, or a fallen bird's nest.

◆ Each child gets a window where she can hang things she likes such as sparkling things that reflect rainbows of light.

Me and My Tree

There are many who say that trees, like humans, have spirits. In this game, you adopt a tree to be your friend.

DIRECTIONS

Whether you live near a forest or a park, pick out a tree that you and your child especially admire, or each of you find your own special tree.

◇ Give your tree hugs.

◇ Have conversations with it.

◇ Sit at its base with your back against it and feel at peace and loved.

◇ Leave it a little present, such as a flower.

◇ Pour water at its base.

◇ Listen quietly within to hear any messages from the tree.

◇ Take a nap under your tree.

VARIATIONS

◆ Increase the awareness that we are part of nature. We are made up of the same energy and have similar designs. Look for the ways the patterns on our body are also in nature.

Examples

◇ Whorls on the bark of a tree like the whorls in our fingerprints.

◇ Spirals in some flowers like the ones in our ears.

◇ Branches of a tree like the patterns of our central nervous system and circulatory system.

♦ Make a rubbing of a pattern.

♦ Make a drawing of the pattern in nature and the pattern in the body.

♦ Make a drawing of your tree.

♦ Pretend to be a tree. Putting down a tap root is a good way of centering your energy and feeling calm.

◇ Imagine a tap root going from your tailbone all the way into the center of the earth, securely holding you.

◇ Make your arms into branches that reach up toward the warmth of the sun.

◇ Gently sway from side to side as if a lovely breeze were blowing.

Young Ones

Gravity Glue

My niece Anna has had fun doing this activity when she's outside on a starry night. It's a way to really experience being part of a larger universe.

DIRECTIONS

Lie outside with your children on a starry night. Talk about the notion that we are just stuck to the side of the earth with gravity glue.

Imagine that on the other planets out there are other friendly people stuck with gravity glue to their planets.

See how the dark sky is kind of like an air ocean. All our planets are like bobbing ships, and really, we are only separated by distance.

Wave at the others!

Harvest Inventory

"What a wonderful life I've had. I only wish I'd realized it sooner."

—Colette

DIRECTIONS

One day, for no particular reason other than to make a good day even better, count off on your fingers, with your child, the number of things in your lives that you appreciate either just today or on all days.

See how many you can come up with.

Example

1. Me
2. You
3. Grannie
4. Fido
5. Comfy home

6. The weeping willow tree
7. Next door neighbor
8. I had a good dream last night.
9. Our cat had kittens.
10. We had a delicious breakfast.

VARIATION

♦ At the beginning of a day that you're spending together, start counting the times that something good happens. Look at each other and say, "That makes twenty-seven things now!"

Young Ones

The "Firsts" Book

No matter what our age, there is always the opportunity to do something for the first time. For an older person, it might be getting her first e-mail. For a kid, it might be getting his first taxi ride.

DIRECTIONS

Keep a separate notebook for all the things you are doing for the first time. Record even the little things. You and your family might find that you go out of your way to do new things just to put them in the book. Doing new things makes more ways for joy to enter.

Materials

notebook and pen

Examples

◇ First time I made a milkshake by myself

◇ First time I made my own plane reservation

◇ First time I volunteered information in class

◇ First time I told a friend I felt hurt by her comment

VARIATION

♦ Make a Book of Tiny Victories. Keep track and celebrate all the tiny victories that happen daily. Dinnertime could be a good moment for each person to tell one of their tiny victories for that day.

Examples

Today's Tiny Victories

◇ Found socks that match.

◇ Got to the bus on time.

◇ Favorite stall in the bathroom was available.

◇ Dog didn't eat the homework.

The Royal Family Takes a Walk

On your next walk, pretend that you are the Royal Family.

DIRECTIONS

When you are walking around the neighborhood, the park, the town, or the forest, pretend you and yours are the king, queen, prince or princess of all you survey.

Look and notice how "your" people and the kingdom are doing.

◇ Are there sufficient places to find food?

◇ Do the roads need tending? (Make a note.)

◇ Are the lawns well manicured?

◇ Are the birds singing nicely? (Have a little talk with them, if they're not.)

◇ Wave grandly at your subjects. (The official Royal Wave can be thought of as a windshield wiper wave.)

VARIATION

◆ See yourselves as the steward of the land around you. You are in charge of making sure the rocks, plants, animals, and neighbors—including spiders, ants, and beetles—are all doing well.

◇ Say little prayers.

◇ Say hello.

◇ Sing them songs.

◇ Leave bread crumbs.

Instant Living Room Volleyball

I work and play with children who have special needs. If I am doing a home visit, there are often brothers and sisters and cousins at the house who want to play, too. Sometimes, my toys will just be a length of rope and a balloon so that we can all have fun together and play instant living room volleyball!

DIRECTIONS

String a piece of rope between a stable object on one side of the room and a stable object on the other side. The height of the rope depends on the size of your players. Lower is always easier.

Form teams with one team on each side of the rope.

Use a balloon for a volleyball and bat the balloon back and forth over the rope.

Keep the rules loose. The only rule is to have as much fun as possible.

Materials
rope, balloon

VARIATIONS

♦ When the children get tired of the game, take the rope down and stretch it out on the floor. The game is to jump over the rope. Jump forward. Jump sideways. Jump backward; hop over with one foot. Then hop over using the other foot. Jump and twirl over the rope.

♦ If you have someone to hold the other end of the rope, keep making it progressively higher so the players have to jump higher each time to clear the rope.

♦ Have players take turns going under the rope while you make it progressively lower. Pretend the rope is "hot" so they have to go really low to clear it and be careful not to get "burned!"

♦ Play around with other ways of holding the rope. If you jiggle it so it wiggles like a snake, they have to jump over it without the "snake" touching them. If you gently swing it from side to side, they get a chance to learn elementary rope jumping and practice the skill of timing.

Middle Ones

There Will Never Be Another Moment Like This One

Help your child realize the preciousness and uniqueness of each moment with this game.

DIRECTIONS

When walking down the road, start noticing all the things that will be different the next time you walk down the street. It is a way of seeing how each moment can never be duplicated.

Examples

◇   That flower will not be at the same stage of blossoming.

◇   The grass will be a little longer (or shorter if it's cut).

◇   That car with those people in it will not come by again and see us as we are right now.

◇   The person walking by will be having whole other thoughts on another day.

◇   That child will be more confident about riding his bike.

◇   That baby will be older and already know more tomorrow.

◇   I will have had more experiences and the next time I walk down this street, even if it's tomorrow, I will be a little different.

Middle Ones
and
Older Teens

Can You Guess Who I Am?

A friend of my youngest daughter taught us this game one evening when she and some pals came to visit. It was such a fun way to be with people that I have since taught it to others.

DIRECTIONS

There are three rounds to this game.

Before the game begins, give each player five slips of paper. On each slip, each player writes the names of a different animal or person, fictitious or real. It can be a famous person or local person whom probably every player is likely to know. The slips of paper are put in one container.

Round One

The first player stands, takes one slip of paper, and, without saying the name on the paper, describes this person or animal.

Example

"He's got really large ears and hangs out with Goofy."

When the others guess Mickey Mouse, he puts that slip of paper into the other container. The next player picks a new slip from the first container and describes the person, and so on until all the slips have been described and guessed correctly.

Materials

pen and paper; 2 different containers, such as a basket and a bowl, or a hat and a box

Round Two

Using the *original* slips of paper that are now in the second container, the first player picks out any slip and can only say ONE word. The others have to guess from this one-word description.

Example

If he got the Mickey Mouse slip, he might say one word: "EARS!"

The other players, remembering that Mickey Mouse was one of the answers, guess correctly.

The slip of paper is put back into the original container.

Each player takes a turn until all the slips have been guessed.

Round Three

Same slips of papers with the same names, except this time *no words,* only mime.

Example

Player mimes ears on his head.

Of course the game can be as simple or as complex as you make the names.

You can divide the group into teams and do it competitively, if you want, and give out points.

All Ages ✓ ～ ✓ ～ ✓ ～ ✓ ～ ✓ ～ ✓ ～ ✓ ～ ✓ ～

The Offering Walks

When you take a walk in Bali, you might have to step over a little offering of rice that someone has placed on the sidewalk in a tiny, woven Pandanas-leaf basket. A little offering left on a sidewalk in your neighborhood would be just as delightful to encounter.

DIRECTIONS

When walking with your child, keep an eye out for ways to create little offerings you can leave behind. It helps you both stay present in the moment and puts an emphasis on appreciating life. You can make a ritual of giving the same offerings on each walk or you can be spontaneous, choosing whatever you happen to see along the way.

The offering can be an object or it can be a movement like a salute or a curtsy.

Materials

found objects, such as a flower, a stone

Examples

◇ Put some grain at the foot of the trees where squirrels scamper.

◇ Place a lovely stone on a large rock you both like to climb on.

◇ Lay a flower on a statue's pedestal.

◇ Curtsy respectfully to a large and ancient tree.

◇ Pick up the trash that mars a beautiful site.

Create Your Own Ritual

When my daughter Marissa got her first period, it was blackberry season. Her godmothers and I were sitting around with her and munching from a bowl of berries as we talked about our own first menstrual experiences. Spontaneously, one of her godmothers decided to "anoint" Marissa's forehead with blackberry juice. Soon we were all laughing and anointing each other! Our faces tattooed with purple berry stains, we looked and felt like a tribe. Perhaps a Sisterhood in Fertility? We didn't name ourselves, we just enjoyed the feeling of connection.

Then, a few years later, when another daughter in our group began her menses, we did a Berry Anointing Ceremony as if it were, of course, the correct and usual ritual.

DIRECTIONS

Make a list of occasions your family could celebrate. Remember that there are many kinds of events that call out to be celebrated. Be sure to add to your list a coming of age, a wonderful experience, a getting over of an illness, and any good news. Whenever you think, "This is a cause for celebration," it's a good time to celebrate. Make up ways to express your joy and hope.

Materials

anything you want

Examples

◇ For a birth in the family, have a decorated egg hunt. Decorate the eggs to suit the occasion.

◇ For getting over an illness, gather gifts from nature—a feather, a pretty rock, a special shell. Put your gifts in a pretty box for the recovering person.

◇ For a coming of age, design a scroll that declares the day a holiday.

◇ For a good report card, make an elaborate favorite treat.

◇ For any good news, dance the polka!

◇ For an anniversary, visit a favorite place.

◇ For a graduation, write a special song.

All Ages

Do a 360

One day I was on a beautiful beach with my young friend Mark, and he said, "Do a 360." We both slowly revolved around in a 360-degree circle, admiring the view from each perspective.

DIRECTIONS

Next time you and yours are in a beautiful spot or even in your own back yard or home, say, "Do a 360" and *slowly* turn in a complete circle, taking the time to admire all that you see at each moment of the turn.

VARIATION

Stand back-to-back with each other. Lock elbows, if you want, and turn together. Take turns calling out the loveliness seen.

"I see that soft yellow blanket I love."

"I see the picture I made myself."

"I see Rags thumping his tail."

Chapter 3

WHEN I DOUBT MYSELF

My Name Spells Wonderful

"God asks only that you include yourself among those you love."

—*Neal Donald Walsch*

Appreciating oneself is crucial to appreciating others. If we help our children to learn to love themselves or never to doubt themselves, we give them the best gift there is. If we truly love ourselves, we can love all of life.

DIRECTIONS

Have your child write out her name in big block letters on a piece of paper. Beside each letter of her name, ask her to write (or you write for her) a quality of hers that starts with that letter. (You don't have to be too strict about starting with that letter. It can just contain that letter, as in the example below.) Decorate the page.

Materials

paper and pens

Example

JENNY

J is for Joyful

E is for Entertaining

N is for Nice

N is for Never tells a lie

Y is for doesn't Yell when she sees a spider or even when she's mad

VARIATION

♦ Make one for every member of the household.

Young Ones

I'm a Work in Progress

To help children learn that they are works in progress, play this "yet game."

DIRECTIONS

Add the word "yet" to any negative assessment children express of themselves or other people. Make up all sorts of things that can't be done . . . yet. Then remember to use this game when your child is discouraged and needs to be reminded of "yet."

Examples

"I can't do long division . . . yet."

"I can't hit a home run . . . yet."

"I am not a famous movie star . . . yet."

"I can't sail a sailboat . . . yet."

"I haven't gone to the moon . . . yet."

"I can't do brain surgery . . . yet."

What I Know So Far

When your child is in an "I can't" mood and needs a confidence boost, or is feeling insecure about performing in a future event, or when you want to engage his attention in order to calm him down and get him to focus, this is a good game to use. We all like to hear about ourselves and especially about our accomplishments. With the young ones, the amount of things they have already accomplished is astounding.

When your child is feeling insecure about her abilities or a future event, sit down with her and make a list of all the things she has learned since she was born. Remind her that stumbling and falling are part of learning. Ask your child to think of a toddler she has seen who was just learning to walk. Did she think the toddler wasn't doing well if he fell? Open your child to the idea that she will continue to be more able as she grows. We all stumble along the way.

DIRECTIONS

Make a list, either by writing it down or counting on your fingers (and toes), of all the things the child has learned since she was born.

Materials

pen and paper

Possibilities for the list are:

◇ Went from an infant who didn't know how to do anything physically to someone who can: walk, jump, hop, skip, run really fast

◇ Rides a tricycle all alone

◇ Says many, many words (in more than one language?)

◇ Knows the way home from the store

◇ Knows the names of all these people

◇ Can brush her teeth and wash her face without any help and so on and so on

Remember to add things that are unique to this child's life such as

◇ Helps Mommy take care of Grandma

◇ Helps your little sister get dressed

◇ Helps Daddy hammer in nails

Young and
Middle Ones

A Passing Cloud Story

When a cloud passes in front of the sun, everything gets dark for a while and it seems that the sun has gone away. Then the cloud passes and the sun comes out again.

When my friend Jane's daughter was six, she went into a brief clinging stage. Having so recently become an independent five-year-old, at six she was having a last gasp of childhood and wrapped herself around her mom "like a limpet" whenever Mom needed to go someplace without her.

When Jane confided to her daughter that she once felt like that with her own mother, the child felt better and Jane did too.

DIRECTIONS

When your child is having a difficult feeling, search through your own memories and find a time when you felt that feeling. Talk about your experience.

Example

"I know how you feel starting at a new school. When I got my first job, I was so nervous the first day that I hid in the bathroom during my ten-minute breaks because I was too shy to talk to anyone. The next day I felt a little braver, and by the end of that week I'd made three new friends!"

VARIATION

◆ Draw a picture together of the sun being covered by a cloud, with trees and animals in the picture dark, and maybe a child crying.

Now draw another picture of how it will look when the cloud passes and the sun shines once more. What will the child in the picture be doing then? Help your child understand that nothing lasts forever, good times or bad times, confusing times or clear ones—all move on. The certain thing is knowing that the sun will always shine again.

⌐ ⌐ ⌐ ⌐ ⌐ ⌐ ⌐ ⌐ ⌐ ⌐ ⌐ ⌐ ⌐ ⌐ ⌐ ⌐ ⌐ ⌐   Middle Ones

Choices, Choices Everywhere

"Feeling is the language of the soul. If you want to know what is true for you about something, look to how you're feeling about it."

—*Neal Donald Walsch*

When my daughter Marissa was young, she heard an adult being annoyed with himself over something he had done. She said:

"He doesn't know if something is done, you can't undo it and even if you could go back in time, you'd still have the same mind you did then and you'd do the same thing again. If you blame yourself, others will blame you, too, and it's not your fault. Just don't blame yourself and don't blame others and the world will be at its best."

I was amazed at her young wisdom and agreed with her. But still, even knowing there is no blame, making choices between options can be very difficult, especially if the pros and cons are about equal.

We used this game in our home to help the decision-making process by letting our feelings guide us.

D I R E C T I O N S

If you have two or more options, say each one aloud with firm conviction as if you have *definitely* made a decision.

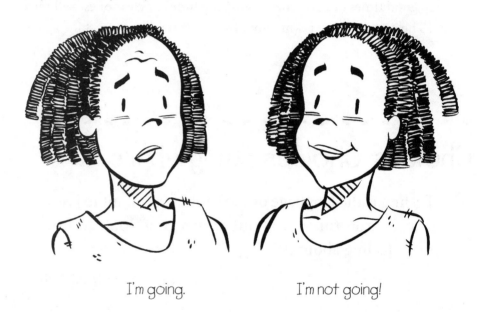

I'm going.   I'm not going!

Example

Say "I am going to go to the party!" Then check on how this makes you feel. Positive (Excited? Happily anxious? Thrilled? Relieved?) or negative (Dread? Stomachache? Nauseous? Sad?).

Next make the same definite statement about the other option.

"I AM DEFINITELY STAYING HOME AND NOT GOING TO THE PARTY!"

How did *this* statement make you feel? If the idea of going somewhere first makes you feel scared but the idea of *not* going makes you sad, then see the fear as a form of excitement. Or remind yourself that being brave is being scared and still going forward.

Go for the decision that gives you a positive feeling, for this is more in accord with who you are and what you really want.

And however it turns out, remember: no blame.

Every Thing Talks a Story

Every object has a story. Sometimes it amazes me, having lived in the same house for thirty years, how many stories there are about the objects in our house. A book, page by page, of the meaningful objects in your life, becomes a kind of biography and gives children a sense of their own history.

DIRECTIONS

Look around your house and pick out an object to write about.

On a sheet of nice paper, write down the story of how this object came into your life and any good feelings connected to it.

Draw a picture of the object or take a photograph.

On another day, pick another object.

Materials

pen, paper, and home objects

Memory Jar

This idea is, I am told, from the early 1900s. Every time a piece of pottery broke, the shards were glued to a jar, making a beautiful mosaic jar full of family memories. Here's a modern version.

DIRECTIONS

When a favorite cup breaks or a sentimental piece of jewelry is unfixable or your child doesn't know where to put that special pebble and seashell, suggest making a Memory Jar.

Get an old ceramic vase or glass jar or clay flowerpot. Secondhand stores and gardening shops are good sources.

Glue the mementos to the jar, using tile mastic for ceramic pieces or any strong household glue for lightweight objects.

Materials

sentimental objects, jar, and glue

The entire surface can be covered with objects overlapping, or the jar can be painted first with enamel paint and the objects spaced evenly apart.

VARIATION

♦ If only ceramic pieces are used, smash the shards into flattish small pieces with a hammer. Glue the pieces on, putting them close together but leaving a tiny space between each piece. After the glue has dried, smear grout all over the shards. After about a half hour, wipe the grout off the face of the shards. You can buy grout in different colors or you can paint the grout after it is dry.

All Ages

The Thank Bank

Going to bed with appreciation on your lips is akin to saying your prayers.

DIRECTIONS

Make a Thank Bank out of a little box with a slit on the top. Decorate the box, if you want.

Every night before your children go to sleep, ask them to think of any thing that happened that day that brought them the gift of a smile.

For everything they think of, have them say "Thanks" and put a coin in the Thank Bank.

Eventually, they can use the money any way they choose, such as buying a gift for someone they appreciate—including themselves.

Materials

a small box and coins

VARIATIONS

♦ Don't use a bank, but just talk about the good things that happened that day as part of the regular bedtime ritual.

♦ Use marbles in a jar instead of coins in a bank. When the jar is full, do something wonderful.

♦ Add beads to a necklace-length string. After a while you will have a joy necklace to wear.

♦ Paste a star sticker on a calendar for each passing day. Add more than one star for a really great day.

All Ages

Say Something Nice Day

A soft-spoken friend of my daughter's told me her story of feeling horribly shy as a young girl, almost paralyzed with fear that no one would like her. She decided that the way to get past her fear was to notice what it was she liked about others and quietly tell them. It changed everything for her, she said, and she never had a problem making friends after that.

DIRECTIONS

We all need practice in saying positive things to each other. On Say Something Nice Day, you notice something you like about a person and tell them.

Declare that this is Say Something Nice Day.

Each player promises to approach one person that day and finish this sentence:

"One of the things I like about you is_____."

When you are back together at the end of the day, you all share your experiences.

You've Got Mail

Sometimes it's hard to give a compliment. Maybe the person can't immedi-ately take it in and rebuffs your praise. Or you worry that the receiver will think less of you. ("If I tell her she is great, will she think that she is greater than me?") Yet we all know how nice it is to be noticed and appreciated and complimented.

DIRECTIONS

Set up private "mailboxes" for each member of the family. You can use shoeboxes or empty tissue boxes or cut empty cereal boxes in half and stack them.

Materials

paper, pen, and small empty boxes

Have a pencil and a pad or supply of scrap paper nearby. Label or dec-orate each box so you know whose it is.

Whenever someone has something nice to say about another person, she writes it down and puts it in that person's mailbox.

Accentuate the Positive Calendar

"We have the freedom to choose one's attitude in any given set of circumstances."

—*Viktor Frankl*

One time my family moved to a foreign country because I had a year-long working contract. Our first months there were a little shaky because the house we were expecting wasn't ready, the schools didn't seem promising, and we didn't recognize much of the food at the grocery store. On the other hand, there were some positive things. We found a good car. There was a beautiful beach. We met some good people.

To keep our spirits up, at the end of each day we would write on the calendar something good that had happened to us that day. It really helped us to accentuate the positive and focus on all the things that were going right.

DIRECTIONS

◇ Every day at the end of the day, write down one thing that happened that made you or your child smile or gave either of you even just a moment of pleasure.

◇ Relive that moment. Talk about it.

Materials

calendar and pen

Just Do It!

One day when I was in a particularly lousy mood, I sat in front of the water because I had told myself that it would be good to go swimming. I didn't really want to but, finally, I did it anyway. It helped a little. Afterward, since I was at the water's edge anyway, I took a walk. It helped me a little more. Then I sat and watched the sunset. By the time I got back to my car, I could hardly remember feeling bad in the first place.

Often there are things we like to do but somehow don't get around to. And then when we do, we say things like, "We really should do this more often," and then don't.

This game reminds us to Just Do It *and then do it some more.*

DIRECTIONS

Materials

whatever is needed

To help players realize the kinds of activities that would make them feel good, have each list ten things that she or he would love to do and hasn't done in months—or ever.

Pick one of those things and make a definite plan to do it. Make reservations if needed, call a friend to accompany you if you like, purchase any necessary materials.

Mainly, make the arrangements, mark it on the calendar, and have a "just do it" day.

Examples

◇ If you have always wanted to play with clay, buy a hunk of clay and for one month make every Wednesday evening "Play with Clay" time. Don't back out and cancel on yourself. Just do it and see where that new habit leads.

◇ If swimming is a source of pleasure for you, remember to give yourself time to do it. Take enough time to just get past a bad mood and begin to notice how soft the water feels or how good your body feels propelling forward through it.

◇ If you have lived in an area almost all your life and have never been to the local tourist spot, whether it's the top of the Empire State Building or a remote cave, make a date and go!

◇ Do something that you have never done and maybe never thought you could. Go white water rafting? Join a painting class? Take up the ukulele? Try out the climbing wall at the gym? Just do it!

Circle of Delight

I've played this game with very different types of groups: daughters, small groups of women friends, and as part of my international workshops where we all barely spoke a common language and had only known each other for a day.

It always seemed easy for people to find something good to say about someone.

When a good aspect of you is mentioned that you didn't know you had or didn't know was appreciated, it can feel especially nice.

DIRECTIONS

The group stands or sits in a circle with one person in the center. Each person takes a turn saying something they appreciate about the person in the middle.

Each person gets a turn to be in the center as the object of delight.

Examples

◇ "You listen to me."

◇ "You make me laugh a lot."

◇ "I am comfortable in your company."

◇ "You seem to have a calm way of being."

◇ "I like the way you cook spaghetti."

◇ "You're a fast runner."

◇ "You look so nice in blue."

VARIATION

♦ Instead of a sentence, say just one word that describes that person to you.

Examples

◊ "Elegant!"

◊ "Loyal!"

◊ "Fun!"

All Ages

Chalking on Rocks

One of the pleasures of making something out of sand is the underlying aware-ness that it is temporary; there is no pleasure for perfection, for the joy is in the doing and not in a permanent finished product.

Chalking on rocks has a similar benefit. Sitting quietly and making whatever marks or drawings inspires you in the moment, whiles away the time, and puts you in a calmer space.

DIRECTIONS

Materials

rocks and chalk

When you are walking with children and stop for a rest, look around for some rocks. Plan ahead and bring some chalk with you, but if you forgot, you will often find that writing on a rock with a smaller piece of another rock produces a chalklike mark.

Play around with making different kinds of marks.

Examples

◊ Emphasize the cracks and lines that are already in the rock, mak-ing an abstract design.

◊ Connect the lines together and see what picture forms. Does it look like an animal, for example?

◊ Draw something that pleases you, like a flower or bird.

◊ Draw a series of pictures on different rocks that tell a story when laid out in a row.

Chapter 4

WHEN I'M SAD

◯ Young Ones

I Spy Something to Love

No matter what the problem is, the answer is always love. In this game, children see something they love and others have to guess who or what it is. Don't stop playing until all children get this chance to feel loved.

DIRECTIONS

A player looks around and spies something that makes him feel love and says, "I spy something to love that starts with the letter ___."

The others have to guess who or what it is.

VARIATIONS

♦ Players identify what is making them feel love by the quality.

Example

"I spy someone to love who is very kind to animals."

♦ If the game is played in a classroom or at a gathering, players identify the person loved by the color clothes being worn.

Example

"I spy someone to love who is wearing red."

♦ The game can be played throughout the day: at the store, on a bus, or while walking down the street. Have your intentions be to notice everything that you are loving right now. The players look around for something or someone that makes them smile and use that for the object of their loving heart.

Example

"I spy with my loving heart something that is round and soft." (It's a bunny in the pet shop window.)

   "I spy with my loving heart something that has gray." (It's the smiling gray-haired lady in the store.)

Young Ones

Betcha Can't Make Me Laugh

This is a tried-and-true game that kids play with each other. Even a sourpuss will lighten up.

DIRECTIONS

One player says "Betcha you can't make me laugh." The others come up to him one at a time and see if they can be so silly that they make him laugh.

   This is a good time to try out one's best silly faces and teach them to each other. Can you do a fish face? Pig face? Monster face? Can you curl your tongue? Cross your eyes?

Whisper in the Wind

When seven-year-old Tyler and six-year-old Jessie heard a news story about people killing each other in a war somewhere, they got very upset.

"Why are they doing that, Mom? Why?"

"Uh, well. Hmmm. Well, actually it's because they want peace."

"They want peace?"

The girls looked at each other incredulously and looked at their mom.

Tyler asked, "Don't they know if you want peace, you shouldn't fight?"

They all sat there feeling powerless to help this situation. Then their mom, Jane, came up with this game: Whisper in the Wind.

They went to the top of a high hill near their home.

"Whisper a message into the wind," Jane instructed, *"and send it where you want it to go. Air travels all around the world and holds all the words that have ever been spoken."*

They thought about the message they wanted to send and whispered together, "Peace is the better way. Peace is the better way." They asked the wind to carry it to those people who needed a better way.

"And remember," Jane said, *"since the earth is round, whatever you wish for another comes right back to you."*

Everyone felt a lot better afterwards. They had done *something.*

This is an empowering game to play with our young, but we can let the wind carry our message at any age.

DIRECTIONS

When you or your child wants things to be different or has a wish for himself or another, find the highest peak around, even if it's just standing on a cinder block, and whisper the words into the wind.

Blow some dandelion or milkweed fluff to accompany your words or, on a windy day, send along a leaf or flower petal for company.

Wish those words a safe trip on their important journey.

VARIATION

◆ Send a greeting to someone who is far away, like Grandma. Then phone her later and see if she got the message.

Young Ones

I'm Writing Me a Letter

To help your young ones learn that there are good days and bad days and that like the tide, life ebbs and flows, use the Postal Service!

DIRECTIONS

When your child is feeling upset, have him write a letter to himself all about his negative feelings. Or, if he is too young to write easily, have him dictate it to you. Or have him draw pictures representing how he feels.

Put the letter in a stamped envelope and mail it to him. When it arrives in a few days, have him open it. See if today is a better day. If nothing else, he will enjoy getting mail, and perhaps he will also learn that bad times don't last forever (and neither do good).

VARIATIONS

◆ In the same vein, when your child is having a good day, have her write a letter to herself and mail it.

◆ Help your child mail an "I'm having a good day" letter to a relative or friend.

◆ Keep a Birthday Journal. Each year you and your child write letters to her twenty-one-year-old self so that when she's twenty-one she will always know what it was like to be seven and eight and nine and so on.

Materials

paper, envelope, and stamp

Middle Ones

Love Breaths

There are people and animals in your child's life that are loved. In this game, they are used to get into a better-feeling place. This is a good game to play right before going to sleep or during a time when your child needs perking up.

DIRECTIONS

On an in breath, ask your child to think of a person or animal he loves. On the out breath say the name.

Encourage your child to concentrate on the person or animal he is naming during the entire in and out breath. What does the person or animal feel like? Look like? Act like?

Repeat the same name over again or say different names of anyone who brings fond feelings to mind.

Middle Ones

You Draw Me; I'll Draw You

Drawing can be such a lovely way to deal with sadness. Usually drawing with someone is like "parallel play." You each have your own good time sitting near each other. In this drawing game, you relate to each other because you are drawing each other!

DIRECTIONS

Materials

drawing pad and pencil

Sit knee to knee, each with a pad or paper on your lap, and draw each other. Draw each other using different methods:

◊ Draw without looking down at the paper as you draw. Just start at one point of the person's face and, as your eyes travel around the face, make your pencil go in the same direction (more or less).

◊ Draw each other as if you were trees or animals or birds or flowers.

◊ Draw each other with a dark expression, such as disgusted or sad or angry.

◊ Draw each other making silly faces.

◊ Draw each other just as you are.

Memories Are Made of This

"The best way out is through."

—*Robert Frost*

When something sad happens over which we have no control, such as a death of someone we love, we sometimes think that it's best not to think about it too much.

Often the best way of dealing with the sadness is to meet it head on.

When the family dog dies and your child is inconsolable, celebrate what you did have with that animal by making a scrapbook.

You can do the same with people or places that are missed. While my children and I were deeply grieving over the sudden passing of their father, we dug through boxes of old photos and made a scrapbook of him and our time together.

DIRECTIONS

Make a scrapbook of all the memories:

◇ Use photos.

◇ Include written memories of special times.

◇ Add a story about a little idiosyncrasy that may have been annoying at the time but is adorable in retrospect.

◇ Cut out magazine pictures of anything that seems fitting and make a collage on one of the pages.

◇ Include snippets of paper with comments others might have made about that person.

◇ Write down the words to songs you sang together or that the person liked.

◇ Include phrases used or favorite sayings.

◇ If it's a pet animal, include pictures or words about things your child liked to do with it.

Materials

scrapbook,
photos,
mementos

One Door Closes, Another Door Opens

> "When there's a big disappointment, we don't know if that's the end of the story. It may be just the beginning of a new adventure."
>
> —*Pema Chodron*

If your experience in life has shown you that things can get better, that even when something was taken away something good also came, share this knowledge.

Seven-year-old Tyler was upset one day because a friend wasn't able to come over to the house to play with her. A little later on, she got a phone call from another friend inviting her to go swimming—a much more fun prospect.

Five-year-old Jessie was upset because she couldn't go where her sister was going. Her mom suggested she plan the day instead to be what she wanted. She drew up her plans. She drew a picture of a swing to indicate time at the park; she drew a picture of her bike to indicate some bike-riding time and a picture of an ice cream cone to give a yummy end to the day. She presented her pictures to her mom and got her ideal day.

Both sisters had the same experience even though one happened on its own and the other was created. For both of them, one door closed and another one opened.

DIRECTIONS

The game One Door Closes, Another Door Opens is a board game without the board.

Players take one of the apparently bad luck scenarios from the list below and make up good luck endings.

Door-closing scenarios

◇ Boyfriend leaves girl, breaking her heart

◇ Young man breaks leg

◇ Man loses job after ten years' employment

◇ Dog runs away

◇ Couple get lost on trail

◇ Ship sinks

◇ House burns down

◇ Wife leaves husband

◇ Computer won't print out important document

◇ Boss harasses employee

Example game

Scenario: Boyfriend leaves girl, breaking her heart

To ease her broken heart and to fill up her time, the girl learned how to play the guitar. She had a lot of free time now, so she practiced and practiced. She got quite good and started performing in little nightclubs. She began to gain confidence and write songs about her experiences. The one about her lost love struck a chord in a lot of people and got her a lot of recognition and a tour. On her tour she met another musician and they began to play duets together. Eventually they married and had three children, all of whom were musical. They performed as a family and were enormously happy.

All because that guy broke her heart.

VARIATION

♦ Play the Glad Game: When a disappointment comes into your children's life, think of the possible positive things that might come of it.

Example

The school trip got canceled.

I won't have to spend a weekend with that teacher I don't like. I can use the money I didn't spend on that new dress I wanted. I don't have to pack. I have a free weekend to do something else.

Keep an eye out for such positive outcomes and point them out:

"See, if that trip hadn't been canceled, you wouldn't have had the time to have this experience that you enjoyed so much."

All Ages

Joy Juicer Words

One day my friend Patty and I needed to cheer ourselves up, so we took turns saying wonderful words like "magnificent" and "scrumptious" and "mellifluous" until we ended up giggling and feeling a whole lot better.

DIRECTIONS

Take turns saying joyous words with your children or whole family. Any happy word will do. Little children may come up with ones such as "yummy," "lollipops," and "mommy." Teens may use "awesome" and "tubular" or whatever expression is *au courant*.

Examples

Pleasure, delight, enjoyment, satisfaction, ecstasy, bliss, elation, eden, enchantment, paradise, rapture, rhapsody, merriment, mirth, amusement, elation, excitement, exhilaration, gaiety, frivolity, glee, guffaw, happiness, hilarity, laughter, jovial, euphoric, cheerful, exuberant, festive, glad, pleased, radiant, joyful, euphoria, heaven.

Rise Up Singing

When my children were young, we took a trip to Mexico in a VW bus. A rowboat my husband had made was tied to the top. To entertain ourselves on the long ride, we sang every song we knew and learned others from each other. We developed quite a repertoire and used it many times in the years ahead. We even had a couple we thought of as our "family songs."

Singing together always cheered us.

On the most difficult day of our lives, the day we went to the mortuary to say our final good-byes to that wonderful, rowboat-making father, we felt at a loss for words. Then spontaneously we began to sing our songs. The family songs. The silly songs. Even in the midst of that painful moment, singing made us smile.

DIRECTIONS

Make a songbook of the songs you know. Include ones your children learned at school, ones you sang as a child and taught them, songs you learned together, and songs you would like to sing.

Bring out the songbook when everyone is in the mood or when someone is feeling down and low in energy and needs cheering up.

VARIATIONS

◆ Play around with a song: How fast you can sing it? How slow? How loud? How soft? How long can you hold the last note?

◆ Make up gestures to go along with one or more of the songs

◆ Learn official sign language for the words or some of the words by checking in a Signing Exact English Dictionary.

Emergency Relief Box

Materials

index cards and
small box

*On gloomy days, when even the internal sunshine is hard to find, it's time to
take out the Emergency Relief Box! Sit down and take turns taking out a card
and reminiscing. Relive the details and remember the way you felt. Reliving
happy times will give you emergency relief.*

DIRECTIONS

On a day when you and your child are
both in good moods and reminiscing,
draw pictures or jot down a line or
two on separate index cards about
your happy times. Remember to
add pet stories. You just need to
write or draw enough to evoke
the memories. Keep the cards in
a small box. Decorate the box, if
you want, in some personal way,
such as with cut-out magazine
pictures of things that make you
smile.

Examples

"Swimming at that lake where
that funny guy who had that
strange haircut taught us how to
spit watermelon seeds and we had
that contest . . ."

"That yellow bird with the red head
that we saw that day on the railing and
remember how when we were
admiring it, it came closer . . ."

"When Lucy had kittens on my bed and I woke up in the morning to this mewing and . . ."

"Our trip to Mexico and remember when we got lost and ended up at . . ."

"When we went to the beach on your birthday and that little seal kept poking his head out of the waves and watching us."

"When my big sister, Jessica, taught us how to catch salamanders."

All Ages

Blow Your Troubles Away

Sometimes the best way to solve a problem is to blow it up, up, and away. Then sit back and watch because you may be surprised at how things resolve themselves.

DIRECTIONS

Get some bubble solution or use dish soap. Blow your bubbles. With each set, think of a dilemma you've just "blown away." Think of it rising to a wise, benevolent spirit.

Ask this spirit to resolve the dilemma in the best possible way.

Materials

bubble solution

VARIATIONS

♦ Write a problem on a piece of paper and tuck it away in a box. At my house, we call this our "Let Go, Let God" box.

♦ Bury the piece of paper in the earth.

♦ Burn the paper in a bowl, asking the smoke to carry the problem away.

Older Teens   ✎ ❛ ✎ ❛ ✎ ❛ ✎ ❛ ✎ ❛ ✎ ❛ ✎ ❛ ✎ ❛ ✎ ❛

It's Crying Time

The medicine of time, taken by itself, is not a sure cure for pain. What helps is what you do with your time. A therapist who specializes in grief suggests that we schedule time to feel our miseries—a time to cry if we want to, a time to acknowledge some deep sadness about an event over which we have no control.

DIRECTIONS

Suggest to your older child that she can pick a time in the week in which she is going to allow herself to be miserable. In this manner, if she starts to obsess in the middle of something else, she can remind herself that she will be miserable about it later—just not right now.

She can set a specific amount of time (and use a timer), or use a more general schedule—Tuesday afternoon after school, for example, or Wednesday evenings.

The time is used to vent fears and anxieties rather than pretend they aren't there. Wallowing is allowed—sometimes wallowing in one's misery feels like a luxurious and valid indulgence. Or the time can be used to talk with someone empathetic.

VARIATION

♦ End the session by accepting that what is done is done and often cannot be undone, and by making plans for the future.

A Notebook of Good-bye

"When you are sorrowful look again in your heart, and you shall see that in truth you are weeping for that which has been your delight."

—*Kahlil Gibran*

When a friendship changes or ends, it may mean that the relationship has run its course. You've learned what you needed to learn, and it is time to let go and go on.

DIRECTIONS

When your older child is suffering from the inevitable heartbreak that happen when a relationship ends, suggest that he make a Notebook of Good-bye and write down responses to these topics:

◇ What were the joyful times? (Relish them and appreciate that they were part of your life's bounty.)

◇ What were the more difficult times?

◇ Name ways in which you are a stronger and more expanded person because of what you learned in the relationship.

◇ What are you looking for in your next relationship?

◇ What are the valuable lessons learned? Sometimes what we learn is what we *don't* want. It's one of the ways we learn what we *do* want.

Materials

notebook and pen

Chapter 5

WHEN I'M ANGRY

Finding the Grumpy Bug

On those days when your child is grumpy and won't quit being grumpy, it's time to search out the source of the problem. It must be the Grumpy Bug. By the time you finish searching everywhere and catch that squirmy Grumpy Bug and toss it out, the room will be full of giggles.

DIRECTIONS

Make a complete search for the pretend Grumpy Bug on your little person. Check ears. Check armpits. Look down the shirt. Look in the pockets. "Find" it, and when you do, "catch" it and toss it out the window.

Be careful or it may jump out of your hands and land on someone else, and then you're going to have to search them!

Now, quietly go and find the Love Bug. Maybe it is in the flowers. Maybe it is in the soft blankets. Maybe there is more than one and you can each find your own sweet Love Bug.

Handle it gently and then ask your child to put it somewhere on her body—behind her ear, in a pocket, in her heart.

"Can you find your Love Bug?" can be a little shorthand message to your child on other days when she seems to have lost hers and needs help finding it again.

Young Ones ⌇⌇⌇⌇⌇⌇⌇⌇⌇⌇⌇⌇⌇⌇⌇⌇⌇⌇⌇⌇⌇⌇⌇⌇⌇

Grouchy Food

What do grouchy people eat? It's important to know this because you can validate a child's right to have a grouchy or sad mood by feeding him just the right kind of food.

You may find that after you do, you'll have to then figure out what happy people eat.

DIRECTIONS

When your child is in a grouchy mood, say something like:

"It looks like you're in a grouchy mood today. I'd better give you grouchy food. Hmm . . . What do grouchy people eat? Worms, I guess. I'd better make you some worms."

You could actually make some spaghetti (worms) to eat, or you could pretend to eat squiggling worms.

Materials

your choice of food

VARIATION

♦ Sad people might want some blue food coloring in their eggs and lots of water to drink so they have extra for their tears. You have to feed sad people very gentle food, like clouds and dewdrops, so I have found that sad people tend to like pudding for dessert.

Young Ones

Mom's Gone Nuts

One time, when my daughters were squabbling and I needed a way to get them to stop before I joined in, I began to act like a gorilla. I jumped around the room scratching and making monkey sounds. It took them by surprise and changed the mood, and soon we were all monkeying around and feeling better. Humor is a wonderful drug. Laughter releases a natural antidepressant into your body. It's organic and free, an all-natural blues buster.

When my friend Jane's children were bickering, she decided to distract them another way. She went into her bedroom, put a pair of her husband's under-

Materials
your choice

pants on her head, then walked back into the living room and went about her work as if everything was perfectly normal. Her kids were startled and then broke up laughing, and soon they all wanted to wear underwear on their heads. It definitely changed the mood.

DIRECTIONS

When children need cheering up or need to be distracted from a squabble, do something ridiculous and very unparentlike.

Examples

◇ Wear something odd—socks on your hands, shoe boxes on your feet. Act like it's normal. (They *are* SHOE boxes, aren't they?)

◇ Talk in gibberish but act as if you are talking in a normal language. Ask for things or make a statement expressing everything with the usual tone and inflection but using nonsense words.

◇ Make up a silly song.

◇ Skip backward or jump or hop where you want to go instead of walking.

◇ Be an animal. Start barking or meowing or cock-a-doodle-doing. The kids probably will need no encouragement to jump into the game.

Young Ones

Wash That Mood Right Out of the Room

When a bad mood has gotten contagious and everyone has caught it, you can change the mood by washing the floor. And since floors always seem to need washing when children are young, this game serves two purposes. You have messy fun and you get the floor cleaned.

DIRECTIONS

Fill a bucket with warm sudsy water and start mopping the floor. Give others a turn with the mop or provide sponges for everyone. Don't worry about water slopping over the bucket. Let the floor get soaking wet. It's only water. It won't be long before the floor invites little ones to spontaneously get into a game of run-and-slide and have a fun time.

Materials

pail of water, mop, soap, and towels

When the fun quiets down or before things get too reckless, bring out some towels and have everyone start mopping up the water.

Empty the bucket, throw the wet towels in it, send the kids off to the shower, and toss the towels in the washing machine, smiling all the way.

Postpone and Count

Sometimes children don't like to be talked out of their anger. In this game, nobody has to give up the anger, just postpone it for a few minutes and get some relief. The game is similar to the old "Count to 100" trick, but it adds visuals. It helps take the edge off anger by distracting it. After playing this game, children feel better despite themselves.

DIRECTIONS

Tell the angry one that this will only take a few minutes and will give some relief.

Pick something in the immediate vicinity to count.

Examples

◇ How many trees?

◇ How many windows in the building across the street?

◇ How many things in the room start with the letter "C"?

◇ How many rocks or blades of grass?

◇ How many times you breathe in and out in 60 seconds?

VARIATION

♦ Count things that aren't in sight.

♦ Name all your cousins.

♦ Name every type of flower you can think of.

♦ List your favorite foods.

♦ Name all the states starting with the letter "A" and so on.

Appreciation Station

Every time you recognize the love you have, you increase it. Recognizing love is a skill. It improves with practice.

DIRECTIONS

Materials

paper and pen

Pick one or more of the Love Lists below. Keep your Love Lists in a special place in the house—the Appreciation Station—and go there when someone needs uplifting or wants to add new appreciations to the lists.

Love List 1

Both you and your child make lists of all the people and animals in your lives that you love and what you love about them.

Example

> What I love about our dogs.
>
> Casey: I feel safe with her. I love her gentleness.
>
> Kaya: I feel happy with her. I love her friskiness.

Love List 2

List the aspects of life that you love right now.

Example

> I love that every day now is warm.
>
> I love my ukulele lessons.

Love List 3

> List times when you received love unexpectedly.
>
> List times when you unexpectedly felt love for someone you hardly knew, such as the cashier at the grocery store, someone who sat beside you on a bus ride, or a baby you held.

Love List 4

> List three ways you can give love today; then do them.

Examples

> I am going to take my dog for a walk; she loves that.
>
> I am going to put my little sister on my lap and give her a "pony ride." She loves that.
>
> I am going to strum on my guitar for a while. I love that.

‹ ﹀ ‹ ﹀ ‹ ﹀ ‹ ﹀ ‹ ﹀ ‹ ﹀ ‹ ﹀ ‹ ﹀ ‹ ﹀ ‹ ﹀ ‹   All Ages

Laughter Is the Best Medicine

"Laughter is like changing a baby's diaper. It doesn't solve anything but it sure improves the situation."

—*Leo Buscaglia*

Science has shown us that when we contract our facial muscles into a smile, there is an increased flow of blood and oxygen to the brain and endorphins (a biological substance that makes us feel happy) are released.

Making laughing sounds can also release endorphins with the result that you may feel better for no reason at all. Then you may start to laugh for real.

DIRECTIONS

Here are some laugh exercises. Do one or do all, one after another.

◊ Practice doing a laugh that has no sound with the mouth open.

◊ Practice a lion laugh with the tongue stuck out and saying "Ho Ho Ha."

◊ Practice a laugh that makes your belly go up and down ("Ho Ho Ho.")

◊ Practice a grandiose laugh by starting small and getting bigger and bigger.

◊ Laugh and jump.

◊ Laugh and dance.

◊ Chuckle.

Middle Ones   ˊ ˎ ˋ ˊ ˎ ˋ ˊ ˎ ˋ ˊ ˎ ˋ ˊ ˎ ˋ ˊ ˎ ˋ ˊ ˎ ˋ ˊ

Feeling Faces

If I could teach only one thing to a child, it would be "Trust your feelings." Being aware of their feelings can help children avoid harmful situations and seek out experiences that are beneficial. Trusting our feelings means that if something doesn't feel right, it isn't. And if something feels wonderful, it is.

Feelings are our most important guides. Positive feelings mean we are acting in accord with what we truly want.

In order to trust our feelings, we need to be aware of them. We can give our children respect for their feelings by asking, "How are you feeling?"

Some of my daughters' friends liked to hang out at our house and they knew that when they talked to me about their lives, I inevitably asked the same question, "How do you feel about that?" Sometimes they would teasingly mock me ("How do you fee---el?"), but as they became young adults, they let me know many times how much they appreciated my asking. Later, they would even call me from college to talk about their feelings. They knew I was still interested in how they felt.

This game is a way for children to check in with how they are feeling.

DIRECTIONS

ˊ ˎ ˊ ˋ ˊ

Materials

face poster

ˋ ˎ ˋ ˊ ˋ

Copy the illustrations on pages 95–97 showing different emotional facial expressions. Put it on your refrigerator.

Ask your children to show you how they are feeling today by picking out a face that expresses what they are feeling and putting a magnet on it. Use more magnets if there is more than one feeling.

They can do this game with you or by themselves at any time they are trying to figure out what they are feeling. What's important is the practice of being aware of how they are feeling at any moment.

You don't have to "fix" them or "make it better." You can just acknowledge their feelings or you can let it naturally lead to an exchange.

Examples

◇ "Good morning, sweetheart. How do you feel this morning? Oh, I see, you are feeling grumpy. I have those kind of mornings, too."

Angry   Apathetic   Ashamed

Confused   Contented   Cranky

Depressed   Eager   Fiendish

◊ "He did that, huh? How did it make you feel? Want to pick a Feeling Face? Anger? Yeah. I would be angry, too. I hate it when someone is mean to me. It makes me feel that they don't like me even if they really do."

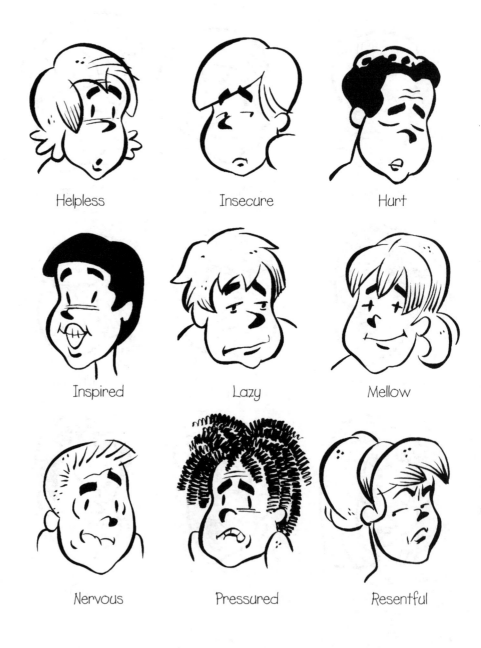

Helpless

Insecure

Hurt

Inspired

Lazy

Mellow

Nervous

Pressured

Resentful

VARIATION

Everyone has their own magnet. When Mom puts her magnet on Cranky, everyone knows to give her some space.

◇ "So today is the day of your play. Which Feeling Face are you going to put your magnets on today? Excited *and* scared. I am excited for you, too. Excitement can be overwhelming and scary. Let's take five deep breaths together."

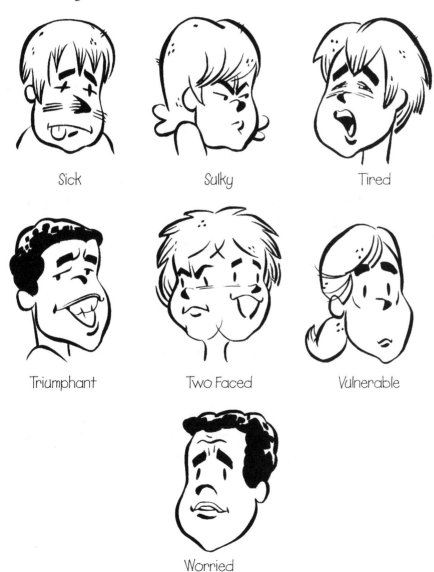

Sick   Sulky   Tired

Triumphant   Two Faced   Vulnerable

Worried

Middle Ones

How Is Your Garden Today?

When we are feeling down, we often can't remember ever being up and don't think that we ever will be up again. We forget that we are whole people with the whole set of emotions and that we will feel differently another day.

Reassure your children that it is human to deeply feel this sadness, and remind them that these sad feeling are only part of who they are, by making a garden representing all their feelings. Since the colors of the garden will change daily, the question "How is your garden today?" can be a way of talking about feelings.

DIRECTIONS

Materials
colored tissue papers, drawing paper, glue, and pens

Cut up small pieces of colored tissue paper. Use a variety of bright and dark colors. Ask your child to think of an aspect of his life and choose a colored tissue that represents it.

Then he scrunches up the tissue and glues it to a piece of paper and draws a stem and leaves under it.

Next he thinks of another aspect or person in her life, chooses another piece of tissue, and makes another flower.

Do as many or few as he wants.

You do the same thing about your life and make your own flower garden.

Note how colors mean different things to each of you. Note the color theme of each person's garden. Is it a bouquet of colors? Mostly one or two colors?

Besides helping a child get unstuck from seeing life in monochrome, doing this game also helps sort out feelings. This is especially helpful when your child is feeling bad and dealing with it by being mean to you.

Examples

◊ Mad at her best friend, she makes one black flower.

◊ He likes his piano teacher a lot and lessons are fun, so he makes a yellow flower for that.

◊ Her dog is fun, and she makes another yellow flower.

◊ Grandma isn't feeling well, so a blue flower represents sad feelings about that.

◊ He remembers the fun time he and grandma had at the fair and makes a red flower for that memory.

◊ She's mad at her best friend's brother, too—another black flower.

Another day, make another garden and notice how the flowers are different colors.

VARIATIONS

♦ Do the game mentally on other days to see what color flowers are in the day's garden. It can be a private way of finding out how your child is doing: "What colors are in your garden today?"

♦ Instead of a garden image, use a pie. Your child colors in the slices according to the feelings felt for that day. "What color is your pie today?"

♦ Weave a mat out of strips of colored construction paper, each strip standing for another aspect of life.

♦ Make a braid of different-colored yarns to wear. Note how the many colors all woven together give it a rich look—a reminder that *all* our experiences make our life full.

All Ages

The Body Is Boss

When I am listening to my body and it says things like "I want to go for a walk" or "I want to eat popcorn for dinner," I can't help but think, "Me too!"

DIRECTIONS

Encourage your child to sit very quietly and listen to her body until it comes up with an idea or thought that makes her feel excited. To help figure out what the body wants to do, make a list of all the possibilities. Cross out the ones that don't appeal and circle the ones that do. Keep eliminating until the right one for now is clear.

Examples

◇ Maybe the body suddenly feels like jumping on the bed, so jumping on the bed as many times as wanted is done.

◇ Maybe the body wants to snuggle and snuggle and snuggle.

◇ Maybe the body wants to go outside and ride the trike, shoot baskets, or gather a bouquet of wildflowers.

◇ Maybe the body wants to do nothing and do plenty of it!

VARIATIONS

◆ Since we all have different bodies that want different things at different times, you could negotiate the day. ("We do what feels right for your body for this much time and then it's another body's turn to decide.")

◆ You might find that your child's body comes up with some things that are surprisingly fun for you to do, too. ("What, lie down and roll down the hill?—me? Uh, but, uh, okay, here goes—Whee!")

Older Teens

How Do You Want to Feel?

As a young woman, my idea of a dream man was someone who could make things with his hands. I was thinking bookshelves. Wouldn't it be wonderful if he knew how to make and put up bookshelves?

What I longed for was to be with someone who was capable and who would make me feel protected.

My husband turned out to be someone who built us a house (and I turned out to be someone who can build bookshelves my own self!).

It's easier to know what you want if you first identify what it is you want to feel.

DIRECTIONS

When your older child is wanting something, such as a summer job, a new girlfriend, or a used car, ask him to concentrate on the *essence* of what he wants rather than on the specifics. Ask him to think about and describe how he wants to feel about the thing he wants.

Then encourage him to feel those feelings as if they were already here. Next, remain on the look-out for the ways those qualities will present themselves. Magic happens!

Examples

◇ "I want a job where I will be part of a team with a feeling of camaraderie. I want to be mostly outside and feel healthy and strong and I want to feel that I am paid enough to have enough spending money all summer."

Older Teens ✦ ✦ ✦ ✦ ✦ ✦ ✦ ✦ ✦ ✦ ✦ ✦ ✦ ✦ ✦ ✦

Finding a Better Thought

"We are disturbed not by things but by the view we take of them."

—*Epictetus*

When things aren't going well, help your child see it as an opportunity to practice feeling better.

One of the most effective skills one can have is the ability to keep finding a better thought. In this game, you try out different thoughts to find ones that bring a little relief.

DIRECTIONS

Make up a set of cards with sentences that can help make you or your child feel better. Use thoughts that were helpful in the past. Even pithy bumper sticker words can work.

When you are feeling low, take out the stack of cards and look through them, finding the ones that are helpful today. You may feel yourself returning slowly to a happier frame of mind.

Example thoughts

I was doing my best.

Not everyone has to like me; my opinion of me matters most.

I may not have the power to make things different, but I do have the power to decide how I will feel about it.

Bad times don't last forever.

When a cloud passes in front of the sun, it eventually moves on.

The only thing we can be sure about is change.

I can learn from this.

At least now I know what I don't want.

She really does love me in her own way.

I can love myself even if I am not perfect.

Life has some interesting challenges.

If I am an eternal being, I'll have plenty of time to do everything.

I can make a plan!

The key to happiness is the decision to be happy.

Nourishment comes from within.

Life is a smorgasbord; follow your taste.

You can look at anything, but you only *see* it when you see its beauty.

No one learned to swim by standing on the shore.

Don't confuse abandonment with challenge. You are not forsaken.

Materials

index cards and pen

VARIATIONS

♦ Keep some index cards blank to be Planning Cards for a plan that you and your child may come up with to help deal with the uncomfortable situation. Sometimes just having a plan brings relief.

Example

Feeling overwhelmed and frustrated by a big spelling list: "I'll give myself a spoonful of vanilla yogurt with cashews as a reward for each spelling word I memorize."

♦ Don't use cards. Just use words that are specific to the situation.

Example

To help with: "I hate my new haircut. I am ugly. No one will like me."

> "I probably wouldn't stop liking someone just because they had a bad haircut."
>
> "I don't think I would want to be friends with someone whose friendship depends on my hairstyle."
>
> "I've had bad haircuts before and finally got over it."
>
> "Hair grows."
>
> "I could buy a new hat that would be fun to wear."

♦ Leave the subject behind and get back to it later after getting in a better mood first by:

◇ Fantasizing about anything wonderful that you wish to have happen

◇ Reviewing a favorite memory

◇ Anticipating a future moment that you are looking forward to

◇ Making a list of things you appreciate about other parts of your life

◇ Getting busy doing something you enjoy

◇ Enjoying being miserable and spending the day in bed!

Chapter 6

WHEN I'M AFRAID

Singing in the Dark

You are probably familiar with the phrase "whistling in the dark" as a way to combat fear. This game has a similar intent, but we sing about the fears!

DIRECTIONS

Help your child make up a song about his fears of the moment. Use whatever melody you want.

"We're worried that the bus is late,

the bus is late,

the bus is late.

We're worried that the bus is late

and we'll be late for school!"

The second verse could go:

"So what if the bus is late,

the bus is late,

the bus is late?

So what if the bus is late?
We'll get there sometime!"

You get the idea. It doesn't have to rhyme or even be a good tune. Just make up the words as they come and keep singing!

The First Step

"Given the nature of life, there may be no security but only adventure."

—*Rachel Naomi Remen*

Every time we do something we haven't done before, we enlarge our sense of ourselves. This expanded sense of ourselves in one area of our lives gives us more confidence in all our abilities. Think of how learning to ride a bike can spark and enlarge the rider's total self-confidence.

If the only thing we can be sure of in life is change, it's wise to cultivate our ability to do new things.

DIRECTIONS

Help your child think of a skill or task that she would like to accomplish. Together think of the first step you could do to accomplish it.

Examples

◇ Child wishes to be able to draw cartoons.

The First Step: Buy a cartooning-made-easy book and practice the examples in the book.

◇ Child wants to learn how to play the guitar.

The First Step: Ask around or keep your eye out for someone who loves to play the guitar, even if they're not professional, and find out if they would be interested in giving private lessons to your child or your child and a friend.

◇ Child wants to make clay pots.

The First Step for the younger child: Buy a bag of clay that will dry in the air or in the oven.

◇ The First Step for an older child: Look for a beginning pottery course at a local community college.

Affirmation Day

Middle Ones
and
Older Teens

I found that affirmations can work even if you don't believe them. Sometimes when I've been blue, I have affirmed "I'm feeling happy, I'm feeling happy" a bunch of times as if it were true and I was just stating the facts. A little while later, I'll notice that I am actually feeling much better.

Don't ask me why it works, it just sometimes does.

DIRECTIONS

Make up affirmations with your child that will speak to what is wanted. Make up some for yourself, too. Decide on an Affirmation Day when you will both practice them many times during that day. You can say them first thing in the morning. You can say them while waiting for the bus or stuck in a line at the supermarket. Leave one tacked on the bathroom mirror or by the door. Plan to think of them every time the phone rings or a car honks or school bells ring.

Compare notes at the end of the day. How was your day affected by your affirmations? If your child had a good experience, he'll have a lifelong little magic trick up his sleeve to use whenever he needs it (and so will you).

Here are some suggestions for affirmations you can use, or make up new ones that exactly state what you wish to accomplish.

They can be general:

◇ I know I can. I know I can.

◇ I am beautiful and strong.

◇ I love life and good things happen for me.

◇ I can handle whatever comes my way.

◇ I am loved.

◇ I choose joy.

◇ I forgive others their faults as I forgive myself my own.

◇ I am open to the highest good for everyone involved.

◇ Today my eyes are open to reasons to feel hopeful.

They can be specific:

◇ I write easily and well. Words flow through me.

◇ I am a fast runner.

◇ I am opening the tap to my creativity.

◇ I can ride my bike.

◇ I can drive a stick shift.

They can be little made-up thoughts that will stick in your mind:

◇ I live a wonderful life with magical ways. Love comes to me all of my days.

◇ I am attractive, strong, and bright. My soul will bring me to the light.

Older Teens

Present Moment/Wonderful Moment

When I start to worry about how the future will be, I use this game to help get me over it. I ask myself, "Well, how am I right now?" Right now I am always okay. My life is not in danger. My belly is full. There's a roof over my head. My children are healthy. By the time I am finished checking in on how things are in this moment, I have let go of the future worries and begun, again, to enjoy the present.

It's my way of following the advice of the Vietnamese Buddhist monk Thich Nhat Hanh, who suggested meditating on the phrase: "Present Moment, Wonderful Moment."

This is a game for parents or older children. Little ones are always in the present, which is why they are so good at being furious one moment and smiling the next.

DIRECTIONS

When your child is worried about the future, distract her from going down that worry road by examining the present moment.

Even when things seem pretty bad or scary, the exact present moment is usually okay. See how many things she can find right now that are pleasant.

Examples

◇ Feel how soft the cat's fur is when you stroke it.

◇ Look at the clouds and notice the shapes.

◇ Cook yourself a favorite food and eat it slowly, savoring each bite.

◇ Find a smell you like such as Mom's perfume or little baby sister's hair and breathe that in.

◇ Say affirmations such as "I feel happy and I am excited about what's next in my life" over and over. Even if it's not true, sometimes it amazingly starts becoming true.

◇ Look around for all the things that aren't wrong. "The sun is still shining." "Everyone I love is healthy." "There are no elephants sleeping in my bed." (Getting ridiculous is great for lifting spirits!)

VARIATION

♦ Stay in the moment by encouraging an awareness of the senses. If you are taking a walk, for example, or just lying around the living room, play this sensory game:

◇ Vision: Name all the things you are seeing. When inside, include details of the rug. Outside, notice details like lichen on the bark of a tree.

◇ Smell: Sniff the air and name the smells.

◇ Touch: Reach out and close your eyes. What are you feeling with your fingertips? If outside, turn in different positions and feel which way the wind is blowing. Feel it on the skin and eyelids.

◇ Taste: Eat things slowly, chewing well and tasting the flavors.

◇ Sound: Be very quiet and listen hard for all the different sounds such as the birds, the wind, the sound of someone walking.

Chapter 7

LEARNING COMPASSION

Be Someone Else

Most parents have had the experience of being told how polite and helpful their child was at someone else's house—putting away toys unasked, saying "please" and "thank you." Needless to say, this same child acts quite differently at her own house. I figured there was only one way to deal with this phenomenon, so I pretended that we were away from home.

My young children were much more courteous when they ate at "Mabel's Home-Cookin' Hash-Slinging Restaurant" than they were at my kitchen table. "Mabel's" was actually just some stools I set up on the far side of our kitchen counter. But at Mabel's, instead of hearing, "She got more than I did," I heard, "May I have some more, please, Mabel?" But, then, Mabel didn't take kindly to fussy children.

They didn't always eat at hillbilly Mabel's. Sometimes they dined at "Chez Babette," with place mats and haute cuisine (sort of). At Babette's, our voices were softer, the compliments more frequent.

DIRECTIONS

Make mealtime restaurant time without leaving home. Make up a persona as a chef or waitperson or cook. Take your child's order ("On the menu is scrambled eggs or scramble eggs with toast."), serve her food, and collect her money. ("What? No money? Have to wash the dishes, then! That's the restaurant's standard policy!")

VARIATIONS

♦ Minor medical problems like a scraped elbow go a lot smoother when the parent becomes "the Doctor" and arms become an Ambulance and the couch becomes the Hospital Bed.

♦ An upcoming trip to the dentist might go smoother if there were a rehearsal. Both parent and child take a turn to be the Dentist.

♦ Parents needing rest are more likely to get it if they take the role of the Sleeping Baby and the toddler takes the role of the Parent.

Young Ones

An Ant's Life

This game provides a fun way to see life from a different perspective and good practice for seeing things from another's point of view.

DIRECTIONS

Sit in some quiet place with your little one and start to focus on the micro-landscape around you and what it would be like to be tiny and living there.

Imagine life in the grass from an ant's perspective. Together, figure out things like:

◇ What are the good places to hide?

◇ Where is a good place for food?

◇ What would be fun to do in that spot?

◇ What would be unsafe?

EXAMPLE

"Ooh, look at how that blade of grass would make a perfect slide. And I could take a nice little bath in that large dewdrop. That milkweed pod would be just heavenly to crawl inside—so soft!"

VARIATIONS

♦ Play the game indoors, sitting on the living room floor. What if you were a mouse? A teeny bug? A giant?

♦ Make up silly questions such as, "If a dragon lived in our house, how would he go to the bathroom?" (Kids really think potty references are very funny.)

♦ Draw pictures of life from another's point of view—for example, an ant going through a giant forest of grass blades.

♦ Pretend that there are elves hiding the next time you are in the park, your backyard or the woods. Look around for good places for them to hide. Have fun gently peeking here and there looking for them.

Young Ones

A Story Like My Story

It helps to hear a story about someone else with the same problem you have, and hear how it turned out. Children like to know that there are others in their situation, whether the situation seems minor (a brother who picks on them) or major (a death in the family).

There is always a story that is exactly like the situation your child is facing if you make one up!

DIRECTIONS

Make up a bedtime story. Have the main character be just the same age as your child. Give her a great name and describe what she is like and what is happening to her.

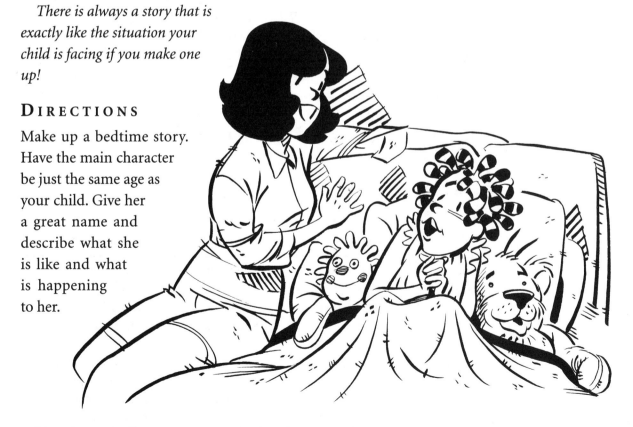

Talk about all the ways that person feels.

Tell what happened to her and how she came to accept or change or resolve the problem.

VARIATION

♦ Go to the local library or school library. Ask the librarian to help you find an age-appropriate book to fit your child's situation, for example starting school, losing a pet, or moving to a new town.

Young Ones

Give Me a Word (or Two)

The people in our lives have different qualities. A person has a quality that is significant for you, but your child may see another quality that is more important to him.

DIRECTIONS

Materials
pen and paper

You and your children each make a list of the people that you all care about. Using only one or a few words, describe each of them from your own perspective.

Example

Person	Parent's	Older Child's	Younger Child's
Joan	Clear thinking	Comforting	Nice to me
Richard	Patient and calm	Loving	Comfy lap
Cindy	Compassionate	Good listener	Plays ball
Lorraine	Alert	Knowledgeable	Soft dresses
Jani	Connected	Interesting	Good gardener
Cheryl	Empathetic	Friendly	Makes good treats
Sarah	Capable	Careful	Pretty drawings
Toni	Fun	Adventurous	Makes good bread
Shirley	Articulate	Smart	Good cook

You Be Me

My young daughters had had a tiff, and we were just sitting down to eat. As we ate, one started making crying noises. The noises sounded forced, so her father and I ignored them. Instead of fading away, the noises got louder, and she ran out of the room.

Later I found her in the garden truly crying. I explained that we hadn't taken her problems seriously because the crying sounded so fake. "What did you want us to do? What would have been the ideal scene?" I asked her, because she was the type of child who was often clear about her emotional needs and tried to train me properly.

She said that she just wanted us to say, "Gee, you feel sad," or offer some recognition that she was unhappy. "I kept making louder and louder noises so you'd notice. You didn't have to do anything about it. Just notice and say so." That very good advice is the inspiration for this game.

D IRECTIONS

When your child is upset and you don't seem to be able to say whatever it is that helps, try reversing roles.

"I don't know what you need. Why don't you be me? If you were the parent in this situation, what would you say or do?"

You may be pleasantly surprised by the answer.

Often, you just need to "notice and say so."

Hang with Birds

Watching birds interact can make for an interesting afternoon. It's fun to notice that birds have personalities, too.

DIRECTIONS

If you see a flock of pigeons at the park, or a group of peacocks at the zoo, or if you have a bird feeder in your yard, notice the interaction between the birds.

Which is the bossy one? Which shows off? Which likes to be alone? Which gets the food the fastest?

Ask your child questions: What do you think the bird is saying? Which bird do you think is the mother? The father? The child?

All Ages

A Garland of Wishes

Materials

construction paper, scissors, pen or pencil, glue, staples, or tape

Did you ever make paper chains? Here's a version that gives children practice imagining happy outcomes and possibilities.

DIRECTIONS

With your child, cut colored construction paper into a pile of 8-by-1-inch strips.

Take turns writing down wishes for yourselves on each strip. Perhaps your child will wish for something specific, such as a new bike, good grades, or new friends. You may wish for something general, such as joy, inspiration, or calmness.

When you've finished writing, it's time to make your chain or garland. First, curl one strip into a circle and glue, tape, or staple it closed. Link the next strip into the first and glue, tape, or staple it into a circle. Keep adding strips until you have a garland the length you want.

VARIATIONS

♦ Make a garland for yourself.

♦ Make a garland for your child. Instead of writing a wish on each strip, write one characteristic that you admire, love, or appreciate about her.

♦ Instead of writing a wish on each strip, draw pictures on some or all of the strips.

♦ Make a chain for yourself, writing one of your own positive qualities on each strip.

At a family gathering or party, have all the guests create a chain of wishes. Give each person strips to put down wishes to add to the chain.

♦ Before your child goes away to camp, a hospital, or any new place, make some of these strips for her, writing down one good wish on each or leaving a few blanks. Put all the strips in an envelope, along with some tape. Your child can chain the strips together and hang them by her bed while she's away.

All Ages

Cairns for Others

Cairns are rocks balanced on top of each other. Building a cairn requires still-ness and concentration.

Materials
rocks or pebbles

DIRECTIONS

Find rocks and pebbles of different sizes. Make a small tower of them by carefully balancing one on top of another.

Wish for something personal by placing a flower petal, leaf, or paper strip with your wish written on it under one of the rocks in the cairn.

The cairn itself can be your wish that all those who see it feel calm and balanced.

Between One and Ten

When my family wants to figure out how much or how little each of us wants something, we give our desires numbers between one and ten: a "ten" if the desire is strong, a "one" if we don't care at all, a "five" if we are feeling neutral. Numbers offer a quick way of communicating preferences, sorting through feelings, and finding the bottom line.

DIRECTIONS

When your children are trying to figure out how important or unimportant something is to them, say, "Give it a number between one and ten." Use your number gauge to answer questions such as:

◇ How hungry are you? (ten is starved, one is not at all)

◇ How much do you want this dress (toy, book, etc.)?

◇ How much do you want to go?

◇ How much do you NOT want to go?

◇ How much is this situation bothering you?

◇ How much does it hurt?

Example

"How much do you want to go to this camp? Ten means you want to go with all your heart. One means you'd rather not, and five means it doesn't matter—you're okay if you go and okay if you don't."

The Talk-Over Voice

In documentaries, there is always a voice that gives us a play-by-play description of what we are seeing ("The lion now lays in wait for the herd to come closer"). I call it the "talk-over" voice. It's fun to use that voice to "explain" things in your own habitat every once in a while. Besides being funny and fun, it gives younger children a model for expanding their language and enlarging their perspectives.

DIRECTIONS

Explain thoroughly, in your liveliest talk-over voice style, what is going on before everyone's eyes. Detail both the obvious and the hidden action.

Examples

◇ Watching the family dog:

"Fido is pretending to be looking at something in the grass but really he is waiting to see which direction we are going to go so he can run ahead and be our leader. Wait, he got distracted by a new dog in the neighborhood and he is cautiously circling the dog to sense its friendliness before he goes in for the big smell."

◇ Watching the family baby:

"The baby is crawling over to the table and he pats the table leg to see if it's strong enough to pull himself up on. He looks around to see if his mother is calm about his plan and since she seems to act like everything is okay, he is pulling himself up. Grunt, pull, boom. He's up and looking around. He sees a corner of the table-cloth hanging down and reaches for it. He sees his mom coming his way looking anxious. Will he have time to pull?"

VARIATION

◆ Take turns being the talk-over voice.

Is That Compliment for Me?

DIRECTIONS

Put each person's name on a separate piece of paper. Give each player one piece. Ask the players to write down something that they like about the person whose name is on their paper. Gather up the slips of paper. Put them into the container.

One at a time, each player pulls one strip out of the container and reads the compliment, leaving out the name of the person it was written about. Others try to guess whose compliment it is. Everyone might call out the same name or different names. The person being complimented is not revealed until all the compliments have been read so that guesses are not based on the process of elimination.

At the end, each person reveals whose name was on his or her paper.

Example

The compliment reads: "I like the way she always finds something good to say about others."

VARIATION

♦ Besides guessing who the compliment is about, also guess who wrote it.

Materials

paper, pen, and container, such as a hat or basket

Walk in My Shoes

This game helps develop compassion for other people.

DIRECTIONS

Take turns putting yourselves into a scene in someone else's life. Imagine how that person would live it. Tell each other or act it out.

Examples

◇ Imagine you are a firefighter in front of a burning building. Flames are starting to shoot out of the windows. What would you do first? How would you protect yourself from burning? What would be your main concerns? How do you think you would feel?

◇ Imagine you are homeless. How would you survive? Look around and notice the best spot to get out of the rain. Where would be a place to get warm to sleep, to find other friends? How would you make money? You don't have to go through garbage cans, but you can look at them and see if there are recyclable cans in them. Where would you find food? If the trash cans are near restaurants, notice if there is food in them.

Other possibilities:

◇ Imagine you are a person with only one arm cooking dinner.

◇ Imagine you are a mother getting seven children ready for school in the morning.

Older Teens

Angel Cards

You can buy a deck of commercial cards called Angel Cards to play this game or make up your own deck. It always feels magical when the card that was picked relates to our present experience. It's also a good way to share ourselves with each other.

DIRECTIONS

Using slips of paper or cut-up index cards, write down various words that describe virtues, values, and delights. Each player picks a card. Then each player says how that word relates to his present situation.

Possible words: Freedom, creativity, expectancy, enthusiasm, patience, love, integrity, discipline, delight, understanding, gratitude, trust, play, beauty, clarity, release, power, honesty, communication, abundance, joy, grace, faith, adventure, obedience, spontaneity, willingness, surrender, efficiency, balance, purpose, humor, responsibility, transformation, truth.

Materials

index cards or paper and pen

Example Game

◇ I got the word "adventure" because I am feeling ready to do something very new and I am thinking of going to summer camp.

◇ I got the word "discipline" because I am having to get ready to study for my midterms.

◇ I got the word "communication" because I am thinking about contacting an old friend.

○ Older Teens

With This Bead, I Thee Bless

When one of my daughters was about to be married, she asked me to think of a ceremony she could do with the women she loved in her life to celebrate this time of transformation.

We made her a magical beaded necklace.

DIRECTIONS

Let each person have a piece of Fimo or Sculpey clay (it's the kind that hardens in twenty minutes in a toaster oven set at 200 degrees). Use different colors if a swirled effect is wanted.

Materials

oven-bake clay and ribbon

While they are kneading the clay to form a bead, each person takes a turn talking about a major transforming time in her own life. The bead can be round or square or a shape that symbolizes her experience.

Each bead holds the best part of each transforming experience.

Cook the beads.

Then, one by one, each person presents her bead that holds the energy of the positive lesson that was learned or the wonderful feeling that was had or the wisdom that was gained.

The celebrant strings them one by one onto a ribbon that will hang in her house to bring her blessings.

Draw Your Symbol for Life

If you had to draw a symbol for your lives at this moment, what would it be? I went to a workshop a while ago in which each person was given a large sheet of paper and some pastels and asked to draw a symbol for what was going on in her life right now. At first, I think many of us felt that this was an impossible task but once we started, it got easier and became fun. The variety of results was amazing. There is no way to do this one wrong.

The magic of it is in the clear seeing of what is important in your life right now.

DIRECTIONS

Using a large sheet of paper and a box of pastels or colored pens, you and your child draw symbols to symbolize your lives as they are now.

Materials

paper and pastels or colored markers

Examples

◇ If a group of friends is what is central in your life right now, along with a wish for romance, maybe a heart with a circle of flowers around it would express that.

◇ If it's a lot of moving around, draw airplanes and trains.

◇ If it's quiet and peaceful with moments of frantic rushing, draw a lake with a storm brewing.

Older Teens ⟋ ⟍ ⟋ ⟍ ⟋ ⟍ ⟋ ⟍ ⟋ ⟍ ⟋ ⟍ ⟋ ⟍ ⟋ ⟍ ⟋ ⟍ ⟋ ⟍

Shadow Cards

"We would never learn to be brave and patient if there were only joy in the world."

—*Helen Keller*

The darkness in life is hard to bear. I appreciated it when an artist pointed out to me that in a painting it is the shadows that bring the painting to life. It is the shading that adds the depth.

This game helps the players find words to help ease the darkness and find other ways to look at a tough situation.

Sometimes just acknowledging that the situation is difficult can help. When my daughter Jessica first had twin boys, she had to contend with those early months of very sore nipples; babies crying, burping, and pooping; and no sleep. What helped her, she said, was she and her husband saying to each other, "This is hard. This is really hard," often accompanied by, "Do you want a hug?"

Materials

index cards and pen

DIRECTIONS

Make up a set of Shadow Cards using index cards. On each card write one of the thoughts listed below.

When life has taken a shadow turn for your child, get out the set of cards and ask him to choose the ones that make him feel better. He can just lay out the ones that speak to him or put them in the order that feels right.

Thoughts for Shadow Cards

◇ Not every day has to be a good day.

◇ I can't choose how I feel but I can choose what I do about it.

◇ It's human to be sad sometimes.

◇ Negative emotions are not to be discarded, just not prolonged. I can acknowledge them and move on.

◇ Today I am just watching, observing, and taking note.

◇ There is something to learn in everything. I only need to breathe quietly, settle into the experience, and watch it with my heart open.

◇ Let it be.

◇ Today may not be what is wanted, but tomorrow may be.

◇ The unexpected can bring joy as well as sorrow.

◇ When one door closes, another opens.

◇ I will consciously breathe in and out ten times.

◇ Misfortune can also bring growth.

◇ Sometimes we get hurt, but bruises will heal.

◇ Whatever happens, I will find a way to deal with it.

◇ Good moments will come again.

◇ I have had some really good moments in the past.

◇ Difficult times show me what I don't want so I can be clearer about what I do want.

◇ Bad times don't last forever and neither do good. I'll wait out the bad and appreciate the good.

◇ Time passes, things change.

◇ This is scary, but I will be okay.

◇ Hope is unpredictable. It can find me in places I wouldn't predict and in people I'd least expect.

◇ Life has a balance. There is no day without night, no light without dark.

◇ Happiness is an inside job.

◇ Sometimes I can't know what is the way until I see what it is not.

◇ Love passionately my miraculous life. Do not wait for a better world.

◇ Nobody can make me feel inferior without my permission.

◇ What another thinks of me is really none of my business.

◇ I have the power to choose how I want to feel.

◇ Nobody ever learned to swim by standing on the shore.

◇ Magic Happens.

◇ The key to happiness is the decision to be happy. I can feel the sadness, but I seek the joy.

◇ A rock in a tumbler gets tossed around and comes out polished.

◇ This too will pass. There never was a night that had no morn.

◇ Is this a catastrophe or a challenge?

◇ Is this a loss or the possibility of a gain? What is the potential gift in this experience?

◇ I learn to love by being in situations that challenge me to be loving.

◇ I will let this emotion flow through me as if it were water on its way to somewhere else.

◇ I trust that every down eventually runs its course. After a while, even a good depression gets boring.

◇ This is hard!

Chapter 8

MAKING MAGIC

Hello Mr. Chair/ Hello Ms. Pot

Give your child the magical sense that everything is alive, even inanimate objects. Disney does this all the time—children love it when the teapot has a face when it's whistling, and the doorknob complains about getting its nose twisted.

DIRECTIONS

Bring life to the things around you by giving them a title and a greeting.

Examples

◇ Start off the day with your child by saying hello to Mr. Sun and thanking it for shining so strongly.

◇ Say thanks to Ms. Pot in which the oatmeal was cooked. ("Hope it didn't get too hot for you.")

◇ Pat the chair and thank it for being so comfy.

◇ Give your family car a name and tell it all the ways it pleases you while you are driving to school.

Continue this game for as long as your child thinks it's fun. Pick it up again when the mood strikes.

Young Ones

Enchanted Braid

Stating our desires helps us focus our energy on what is important to us right now. Wearing this reminder keeps the energy of our wishes with us all day.

Materials

pen, ribbon

DIRECTIONS

Encourage your child to express a wish she has for herself. See if you can discern the essence of what she wants rather than the particulars. She may currently wish to win a writing contest. The essence of her wish, however, may turn out to be for recognition of her writing skills. Help her write the essence of her wish on a bracelet-length piece of ribbon.

Braid the ribbon into her hair or tie it around her wrist or ankle so her wish will stay close to her.

Expect it to come true.

Middle Ones

While You Sleep

Hypnotists use the technique of making a suggestion when the patient is in an Alpha state. It is in this right-before-sleep state that we have less resistance to suggestion.

You can use this technique with your young one just as she is falling off to sleep, when her breathing is slow and regular and her eyes are still (rapid eye movement—REM—shows she is dreaming).

The game is to whisper in her ear something she would like to have happen or a positive affirmation.

This game also lets children know that even while they sleep, you are watching out for them.

DIRECTIONS

Decide with your child some affirmations that she would like you to whisper to her while she is sleeping.

Examples

◊ "Maxwell will have a good time at the new school and make new friends."

◊ "Griffen will wake up knowing what he wants to do for his science project."

◊ "Molly is beautiful."

⌐ ⌐ ⌐ ⌐ ⌐ ⌐ ⌐ ⌐ ⌐ ⌐ ⌐ ⌐ ⌐ ⌐ ⌐ ⌐ ⌐ ⌐ ⌐ Middle Ones

Delicious Dreams

Ignoring all reality and making an outrageous wish for the future can have surprising results. I used to enjoy fantasizing about living on a tropical island. I liked thinking about being in warm water, snorkeling, swimming, boating— and now I am!

Even though I dumped the raft and both of us on our first whitewater rafting trip when my daughter Marissa was nine, she still loved it and imagined being a river guide one day. Now, in the summers, she is a professional guide on wild and scenic rivers.

DIRECTIONS

When your child is unhappy about the way things are now, she can make them exactly the way she wants them in her mind. In this game the child designs the future according to her wildest dreams. It's a bit like "What do you want to do when you grow up," but the emphasis is on indulging in the delicious details and completely enjoying the fantasy. The time spent in this "enjoyment state" will not only give relief from unhappy feelings but also will put her in touch with her dreams.

Ask your dreamer:

"Imagine that in the future, you can be or do anything you want. You get to choose anything. What would it be?"

When you get a response, ask all sorts of leading questions: "What are you wearing?" "Who else is there?" "What do you do?" "What is the best part?" "What is the weather like?" "Can you describe the area?"

Example

If your child says: "I am going to join the circus and fly on a trapeze and the crowds will cheer!"

You then ask: "What will your costume look like?" "Who else will be in the act with you?" "What color is the circus tent?"

VARIATION

After the child has identified his dream, take an action that follows this interest.

Example

He wants to be a cowboy and live on a big ranch and ride the range.
Action Possibilities:

Take him to a riding stable so he can be on a horse.

Go to the library and find books about cowboys.

Get him a cowboy hat.

Enchanted Cloaks Last Forever

Middle Ones
and
Older Teens

When your older child is about to embark on a new experience, family and friends can wish him all kinds of magic by presenting him with fantasy gifts that they think will enhance his life.

There is power in wishes and joy in having the people you love thinking about your needs and wishing for you.

DIRECTIONS

Sit in a circle around the person who is about to have a new experience.

One by one, present him with a fantasy gift that will help him on his journey.

Examples

◇ "I am putting this magical cape over your shoulders to always protect you from harm."

◇ "I am giving you these rose-colored glasses so you will always see the best part of whatever happens."

◇ "I have blown kisses into this box so you will always have my love with you."

Intuition Exercises

The more we use a muscle, the stronger it gets. This is also true of our sixth sense: our intuition. This exercise strengthens this sense and gives us more faith in our hunches. Recently I was wanting a specific used car but couldn't find it. I had a strong hunch to follow a lead to a car, even though it wasn't the one I wanted. Unknowingly, I walked into the wrong building and asked for the person who was selling the car. The woman at the desk looked surprised and said she was going to sell her car but she hadn't put up any notice. It turned out to be the exact model I wanted at a better price than I had hoped for.

DIRECTIONS

Practice with your children the skill of listening to their inner voices by doing exercises like these:

◇ Guess who is on the phone when it rings before you answer it.

◇ Guess which elevator is going to arrive first.

◇ Guess what colors your teacher (co-worker, best friend) is going to wear that day.

◇ Guess who will be the first person you see today.

◇ Guess the number when rolling dice.

◇ Guess the suit when picking a card.

Give What You Want

In a movie I saw, Eddie Murphy played a guru of sorts and had this great line: "If I were you, and I am you. . . ." I thought it was such a clever way of expressing the concept that we are all one. In this game, we decide something we want and then give it to another because if we are all one, then giving to another is giving to oneself.

DIRECTIONS

If your child or you are wanting something, give it to another. Do something that would give the very thing you want to someone else

Examples

◇ Wanting serenity: Spend quiet time with someone. Read him a story or go for a lovely walk. Bolster the feeling of serenity.

◇ Wanting love: Give love to someone. Spend extra time playing with a pet. Think of a perfect present to bring someone. Visit someone who would want a visitor.

◇ Wanting help: Do something very helpful. Help a busy mom with her kids or help her clean her house. Go to the grocery store for an elder. Relieve someone who is taking care of an ill person.

◇ Wanting money: Give money to someone who needs it more than you do.

◇ Wanting joy: Send something to someone you care about, such as a pressed flower, a cartoon, a little story, words of love.

Middle Ones
and
Older Teens

Ask for a Sign

Along with asking for what one wants, it's possible to just ask for a sign that you are being heard by a larger, higher power.

One time when I was in a doubting phase, I asked for something specific, because I was about to make a major leap in my life based on the belief that a higher loving power would guide me in the right direction.

I didn't want any vague, namby-pamby sign that could be open to inter-pretation. I wanted something clear-cut, so I asked for the exact mate to a sin-gle black sock. It couldn't be just any black sock; it had to be the exact mate to one I had lost.

A few days later, even though it was starting to drizzle, I had the impulse to take a walk. And beside the sidewalk I found a black sock—the exact mate. It had a red ribbon around it.

I made that leap and it was one of the best moves of my life.

I encourage my children and friends to ask for a sign when they are in a quandary; the results can be so satisfying.

DIRECTIONS

When you or your child are feeling unsure about something, ask for a sign. Be very specific, as in my example, or more general, such as "Make every-thing go smoothly if I am to go on this trip."

Obstacles to your goals could be signs. Five busy signals in a row could be saying that the time is not right to call this person.

An unusually colored bird singing outside your window can be a sign that everything is going along fine.

A conversation with someone who casually mentions just the infor-mation you were seeking counts as a sign.

When I get chills at the back of my neck or my arm hair stands on end, I figure that this sign is for me!

Be alert!

Magic Collage

Middle Ones and Older Teens

Every New Year, when my children were adolescents and teenagers, we made a collage to represent their wishes for the coming year. We would put them up on the wall and be amazed at the end of the year to see how many things wished for actually happened.

I met a woman who said she had done a collage when she was much younger on the subject of what she wanted in her life. She just went through magazines and cut out anything that appealed to her. One of the pictures was a tropical scene with the word "Rota" on it. She had no idea where or what Rota was.

Twenty-five years later, she found the collage when she was cleaning out her stuff from her parents' home in Michigan. She was shocked to see that collage, for she had been happily living on the island of Rota for the past twelve years.

DIRECTIONS

Materials

magazines,
cardboard,
scissors, and
glue

Go through magazines, catalogs, photos, and greeting cards to find pictures of things you would like to have happen or feelings you would like to experience. Only each individual needs to understand his or her own symbolism.

These are your hopes for the New Year.

Arrange them in whatever pattern is pleasing. Then glue them to poster board or cardboard. Add written words, such as affirmations, if you want.

The collage can be completed in one wonderful day of creating, or you can leave part of it blank and add to it later.

Put the collage in a prominent place for a continual reminder of what matters.

Or hide it away and bring it out at the next New Year and see what came true.

VARIATIONS

◆ Instead of New Year's, do it for each birthday.

◆ Have a theme such as "What I would like for my life," "What I wish for the world," or "The qualities I want in my next boyfriend (or girlfriend)." (Don't worry if you get what you wanted and then realize it wasn't what you thought it would be. That just means that *now* you are in a more knowledgable position to make new, probably better, wishes. It's all part of the learning process.)

Doing Your Half of the Magic

Wishing for something but doing nothing can feel frustrating. Empower your wish by doing something that symbolically represents it and you'll be doing your half of the magic.

DIRECTIONS

When you want something, think about what could be done that would symbolically express what is wanted.

Examples

◇ If you want new clothes or toys: Give away clothes or toys that you no longer wear to make space for the new ones when they come.

◇ If you want to do well on an exam: Clear your desk and organize drawers to reflect an orderly mind that will remember the knowledge it has.

◇ When you want to clear out old, unproductive thoughts: Clean out a messy area under the sink, a part of a room where stuff piles up, or cobwebs in the attic—to clean unwanted thoughts from the mind.

◇ If you'd like to get rid of ways of behaving that no longer serve you: Weed the garden. Go through your books and give ones that aren't going to be reread as gifts to a local library or hospital. Throw out stuff that is no longer useful.

◇ To find clarity, clear thinking about an issue: Wash windows. Clean and fastidiously tidy up your room so that you can clearly see what you have.

◇ When you want good news: Dust off the telephone. Wash off the mailbox. Sweep the path to the house. Start the day by saying, "Something good is coming."

VARIATIONS

♦ Hang things on a string that symbolize what is wanted.

Examples

◇ "I am hanging a blue bead today because it reminds me of the ocean when it is calm and still powerful. These are the feelings I want for today."

◇ "I am hanging a dried rosebud because I want to notice the beautiful things in life today."

◇ "I am hanging a toy wheel because I want to find a skateboard buddy."

Made-Up Stories

DIRECTIONS

When you are driving past a car, have a look at the driver and passengers in the car and notice the kind of vehicle they are driving, and then take turns having a go at making up a story about them all.

Examples

◇ This man has waited all his life for his retirement so that he can go down to Mexico and go fishing. His wife has agreed to go along but her plan is to take that extra car they are hauling in the back and go right to the markets and buy things she fancies.

◇ That woman is rushing to see her boyfriend, but she is torn because she also loves the boy back home and she has to decide which one she loves more. However, at the next rest stop, she is going to meet that guy who just went by in the Mercedes convertible and fall in love with him, too.

Change the Energy

If you are having difficulty with someone, concentrate on all of that person's qualities that you like, and be amazed at what happens next.

I've played this a lot, but most recently with a young girl who was complaining about a close friend. "She never asks me how I am," she said, "she just wants me to listen to how she is."

We spent some time playing Change the Energy by concentrating on all the traits about her friend that she did appreciate. She told me great stories illustrating these good points.

That night when she got home the phone rang. It was her friend and the first words out of her friend's mouth were, "I was just thinking about you. How are you doing?"

DIRECTIONS

Materials
paper and pen

When your child is having difficulty with one person or with a group of people in a situation such as at school or on a job, have her write down on separate pieces of paper all the qualities she likes about each person.

Start with the easiest person for her to like and work her way to the most difficult. Be sincere; there is always something to admire.

On the following days, write down any changes that happen in those relationships.

Middle Ones
and
Older Teens

The Healing Circle

This is a group game that you can all do for someone who is not feeling well and needs some special attention.

DIRECTIONS

Make a circle around the person who needs attention and take turns imagining the best cure. Players tell or act out their images to the person in the center.

Examples

◇ For a person whose skin got badly scraped when he fell, the others might imagine that little elves come along and paper the hurt area with fresh skin the way wallpaper is put on a wall.

◇ For a person who has a fever, the others might imagine her in a lovely snowstorm, with cool, fresh snowflakes caressing her body and cooling her down.

◇ For someone who feels ill, the others might imagine him striding up a mountain on a crispy fall day feeling powerful and strong and very, very healthy.

All Ages

Voodoo a Parking Space

I discovered this game by accident. At the time, our family car was a huge old Lincoln, an atrocious yellow color. We bought it when compact cars were in vogue and those old luxury dinosaurs were cheap. We called it "The Banana Boat" because of its unique color and size. Surely, there wasn't another like it around.

Driving to town through heavy traffic one afternoon, I started wishing for a parking space and imagining our car parked right in front of the bank. Imagine my surprise when I arrived and saw a car absolutely exactly like ours parked right in front of the bank!

Now, I imagine an empty space! I am amazed how often it works.

DIRECTIONS

As you and your child are driving toward your destination, imagine an empty parking space near where you want to go. Or imagine a car pulling away just as you get there, particularly if you are headed toward a parking lot. Have him talk about what he sees in his mind's eye. When you find your parking spot, affirm how close you actually are to his imagined space.

VARIATIONS

♦ Imagine other positive outcomes together, particularly when you have figured out the chances that the outcome you imagine will make someone happy.

Examples

◇ Being at the head of the line

◇ Finding a lost item of clothing

◇ Winning a game of chance

◇ Learning a skill

All Ages

Keeping Track of the Miracles

"There are two ways to live life. One is as though nothing is a miracle. The other is as though everything is."

—*Albert Einstein*

I like to keep track of little miracles, such as coming upon something I have been looking for, running into a person I want to see, getting just the right information exactly when I needed it. The more miracles I notice, the more there are.

Recently, daughter Roxanne was telling me about the miracle of finding a basement apartment to rent near her university. She had been following up on a less desirable location even though it wasn't the place she wanted when she went to the nearest public phone. It wasn't working. She had to go searching for another phone. When she finally found one, on the side of the phone was this notice:

"Basement apt. available. 4 blocks from the university."

She was the first one who called, and she got it.

DIRECTIONS

Keep a Miracle Log available. Whenever something serendipitous happens, anyone in your family can log in by just writing down what happened.

Materials

notebook and pen

Examples

◇ A friend coming over just to play

◇ Meeting a new friend whom you immediately feel a friendship with

◇ Getting tickets to an event that was sold out

◇ Hearing a song come on the radio that you had just been thinking about

◇ Dropping buttered bread and having it land butter-side-up

VARIATION

♦ Include the wish that preceded the serendipitous event.

Examples

◇ Wishing I could find my favorite pen and finding it behind the couch when I went to retrieve the ball

◇ Wishing something exciting would happen and then getting an invitation to go on an outing

◇ Wanting an adventure and then accidentally getting lost on a hike and having a fun adventure finding the way back to the trail

All Ages

Wise Old Woman

Sometimes the answer to our problems is right inside us.

DIRECTIONS

Talk your child through a pleasant meditation. Ask him to get comfortable and close his eyes. Then say slowly:

"Imagine that you are walking through a forest. The trees are large and protective and the ground is thick with years of brush that makes a nice sound as you walk on it. You come to the edge of the woods and find a clear sparkling river that is happily babbling along. You walk along the river edge and feel the warmth of the midday sun. You see a place where a log has fallen across the river, a log that is the perfect size for you to cross over on. You walk across the log and on the other side is a small hill. You eagerly climb up the hill, sensing that something wonderful will be at the top. When you get to the top, indeed there is a lovely little cabin made of tree bark with grass sod on the roof.

"A sweet old woman with white hair and twinkly eyes is standing in the doorway and is so happy to see you. She invites you in and you feel so happy and relaxed in her company. She has a little message for you. Listen to it and tuck it into your heart." (Wait quietly for a few minutes while your child "hears" the message.)

"Now it's time to go. Thank your wonderful friend for her message and say goodbye. Now run down the hill or even roll down if you like, cross over the log, skip through the forest and come home full of your good feeling."

Your child can then tell you what he learned, if he wants to, or he can write it on a piece of paper and hide it away, or draw a picture or symbol of his experience.

Older Teens

Dream BIG

Don't limit dreams. It could limit manifestations. Dream BIG.

DIRECTIONS

Imagine a future. Imagine the best that you and everyone playing this game can think of. Take turns saying your future wish and then, with the help of others, make it even bigger, then bigger still. It's important to enjoy your fantasy the whole time and ignore those annoying little voices that say "But that's not possible." It *is* possible in your dreams, and the magic can lie in all the pleasure you are getting just thinking about it.

Example

DREAM: I would like to have a little boat on a little lake.

BIGGER DREAM: I would like to have my little boat on a little lake *and* a big sailboat so I can sail to tropical islands.

BIGGER STILL: I would like to have my little boat on a little lake and a big sailboat so I can sail to tropical islands *and* have ideal homes in two or more locations.

EVEN BIGGER STILL: I would like to have my little boat on a little lake and a big sailboat so I can sail to tropical islands and have ideal homes in two or more locations *and* have interesting work that pays me more than enough money.

CLOSING THOUGHTS

I play games for a living. My job as an occupational therapist is to go into classrooms with children who have various skill levels and play games with them. The games enhance a variety of skills, such as motoric abilities, self-esteem, self-awareness, and hand dexterity. Even though my intentions are for the children to gain skills, my method is pure fun. I like the children to grin and laugh so they feel good about themselves and about life. This pleasant mood keeps their minds open to learning.

I use the same method to teach adults. My workshops on playing games with children have been conducted in many different places in the world, from Cambodia to Nicaragua to Fiji, to name just a few. I have played with many kinds of people, from Vietnamese refugees to barbwire-enclosed camps to professional teachers and therapists at elegant hotels in California. My last book, *Self-Esteem Games,* was translated into Spanish and Hebrew. Games cross all cultures.

In every workshop, the participants laughed and learned by playing. Whether the players were gray-haired ladies or young sensual women or children in an orphanage, I have found that playing games is a way for everyone to feel connected to each other and open to the joys of living.

In this book I have shared with you the games my family and friends use to turn up the level of joy in our lives. These are games for the heart. Games to keep you loving the preciousness of you. Games to help you get back in touch with the goodness of life.

I feel a spiritual connection to the Source of All that Is when I am joyful, but I don't need that for a reason to make the effort to find the joy. The bottom line is enough: It feels good to feel good.

Index

○ signals activities that are good for groups.

All Ages

Young Ones

Young and Middle Ones

Middle Ones

Middle Ones and Older Teens

Older Teens

For You